VOLUME 17

D0094014

MATTHEW

Robert E. Luccock

ABINGDON PRESS
Nashville

MATTHEW

Copyright © 1988 by Graded Press

This book is printed on recycled, acid-free paper.

Library of Congress Cataloging-in-Publication Data

Cokesbury basic Bible commentary.
Basic Bible commentary / by Linda B. Hinton . . . [et al.].
  p. cm.
Originally published: Cokesbury basic Bible commentary. Nashville:
Graded Press, © 1988.
ISBN 0-687-02620-2 (pbk. : v. 1 : alk. paper)
  1. Bible—Commentaries. I. Hinton, Linda B. II. Title.
[BS491.2.C65 1994]
220.7—dc2094-10965
CIP

ISBN 0-687-02636-9 (v. 17, Matthew)
ISBN 0-687-02620-2 (v. 1, Genesis)
ISBN 0-687-02621-0 (v. 2, Exodus–Leviticus)
ISBN 0-687-02622-9 (v. 3, Numbers–Deuteronomy)
ISBN 0-687-02623-7 (v. 4, Joshua–Ruth)
ISBN 0-687-02624-5 (v. 5, 1–2 Samuel)
ISBN 0-687-02625-3 (v. 6, 1–2 Kings)
ISBN 0-687-02626-1 (v. 7, 2 Chronicles)
ISBN 0-687-02627-X (v. 8, Ezra–Esther)
ISBN 0-687-02628-8 (v. 9, Job)
ISBN 0-687-02629-6 (v. 10, Psalms)
ISBN 0-687-02630-X (v. 11, Proverbs–Song of Solomon)
ISBN 0-687-02631-8 (v. 12, Isaiah)
ISBN 0-687-02632-6 (v. 13, Jeremiah–Lamentation)
ISBN 0-687-02633-4 (v. 14, Ezekiel–Daniel)
ISBN 0-687-02634-2 (v. 15, Hosea–Jonah)
ISBN 0-687-02635-0 (v. 16, Micah–Malachi)
ISBN 0-687-02637-7 (v. 18, Mark)
ISBN 0-687-02638-5 (v. 19, Luke)
ISBN 0-687-02639-3 (v. 20, John)
ISBN 0-687-02640-7 (v. 21, Acts)
ISBN 0-687-02642-3 (v. 22, Romans)
ISBN 0-687-02643-1 (v. 23, 1–2 Corinthians)
ISBN 0-687-02644-X (v. 24, Galatians–Ephesians)
ISBN 0-687-02645-8 (v. 25, Philippians–2 Thessalonians)
ISBN 0-687-02646-6 (v. 26, 1 Timothy–Philemon)
ISBN 0-687-02647-4 (v. 27, Hebrews)
ISBN 0-687-02648-2 (v. 28, James–Jude)
ISBN 0-687-02649-0 (v. 29, Revelation)
ISBN 0-687-02650-4 (complete set of 29 vols.)

00 01 02 03—10 9 8 7 6 5 4 3

MANUFACTURED IN THE UNITED STATES OF AMERICA

Contents

Outline of Matthew

I. Prelude: The Origins of Jesus (1:1–2:23)
  A. Genealogy (1:1-17)
  B. Annunciation and conception (1:18-25)
  C. The birth of Jesus (2:1-12)
  D. Flight into Egypt and return (2:13-23)
II. Discipleship (3:1–7:29)
  A. Jesus begins preaching (3:1–4:25)
    1. John the Baptist (3:1-12)
    2. Jesus is baptized (3:13-17)
    3. Jesus' temptation (4:1-11)
    4. Jesus' early ministry (4:12-25)
  B. The Sermon on the Mount (5:1–7:29)
    1. The Beatitudes (5:1-12)
    2. Disciples as salt and light (5:12-16)
    3. The higher righteousness (5:17-48)
    4. Practicing piety (6:1-18)
    5. Other religious teachings (6:19–7:27)
    6. Summary (7:28-29)
III. Apostleship (8:1–11:1)
  A. Ministry of healing and teaching (8:1–9:34)
  B. Instructions to the disciples (9:35–11:1)
    1. The need for apostles (9:35-38)
    2. Commissioning the apostles (10:1-4)
    3. Directions for mission (10:5-42)
    4. Summary (11:1)
IV. About Jesus and the Kingdom (11:2–13:58)
  A. Rejection by scribes and Pharisees (11:2–12:50)

1. Jesus and John the Baptist (11:2-19)
2. Woe to unrepentant cities (11:20-24)
3. Self-revelation of Jesus (11:25-30)
4. Opposition by the Pharisees (12:1-45)
5. Jesus' true family (12:46-50)
   B. Teaching in parables (13:1-58)
V. The Church (14:1–19:2)
   A. Training disciples for ministry (14:1–17:27)
      1. Murder of John the Baptist (14:1-12)
      2. Jesus' miraculous works (14:13-36)
      3. Controversy over ritual cleanliness (15:1-20)
      4. Encounter with Gentiles (15:21-39)
      5. Warning of Pharisees and Sadducees (16:1-12)
      6. Peter's confession of faith (16:13-28)
      7. The Transfiguration (17:1-13)
      8. Healing the epileptic boy (17:14-21)
      9. Prediction of the passion (17:22-23)
      10. The Temple tax (17:24-27)
   B. Church discipline (18:1–19:2)
VI. Judgment (19:3–26:2)
   A. Jesus goes to Jerusalem (19:3–23:39)
      1. Demands and rewards (19:3–20:28)
      2. Jesus heals two blind men (20:29-34)
      3. Events in Jerusalem (21:1–23:39)
   B. Teaching about the end of the age (24:1–26:2)
      1. Signs of the end (24:1-51)
      2. Parables of judgment (25:1-46)
      3. Summary (26:1-2)
VII. The Passion of Jesus (26:3–27:66)
   A. Conspiracy of priests and elders (26:3-5)
   B. Anointing at Bethany (26:6-13)
   C. Judas' betrayal to the chief priests (26:14-16)
   D. The Last Supper (26:17-35)
   E. The garden of Gethsemane (26:36-46)
   F. Jesus' arrest (26:47-56)
   G. Hearing before the Sanhedrin (26:57-68)
   H. Peter's denial (26:69-75)
   I. Jesus before Pilate (27:1-26)

Introduction to Matthew

The title of the first book in the New Testament tells us the most important thing we need to know about it. *The Gospel According to Matthew* is a book of *good news* about Jesus the Christ. A history book, a book of teachings, a manual for Christian disciples—Matthew is all of these. But above all it proclaims that Jesus is Emmanuel, God with us (1:23); that Jesus is the Christ, the Son of the living God (16:16). Matthew is the first of four such books in the New Testament. We call the first three of these *synoptic* Gospels because they give us parallel accounts of the life and teachings of Jesus, his death and resurrection.

When we are aware of the sources of the Gospel of Matthew, its singular structure, and some of its distinguishing features we can better understand and appreciate this book.

Sources

Matthew cannot be called the author of the first Gospel in the sense that he wrote the book himself. It would be more accurate to speak of him as the *redactor* or *editor*. Whoever Matthew was, he compiled the book from several sources already in existence. To say this in no way diminishes the value of the book, for its importance lies in the arrangement of the material to serve Matthew's purposes. Most New Testament scholars now believe that Matthew gathered the contents of his Gospel from four principal sources: (1) the Gospel of Mark, (2) a collection of the teachings of Jesus, more than likely from an earlier document, also known to Luke but apparently not to Mark, which has long since disappeared, (3) a source from which Matthew gathered material appearing only in his Gospel, some of which may have come from the oral tradition of Israel, and (4) the Hebrew Scriptures, what we call the Old Testament. We will see how Matthew used these sources as we consider the structure of his Gospel and the purposes it served.

Structure

Matthew has been called "The Teacher's Gospel," not surprisingly, because nowhere else are the teachings of Jesus so helpfully and memorably arranged for teachers. Chapters 3-25 are divided into five "books," calling to mind the first five books of the Old Testament, which are called the five books of Moses, and also the division of the book of Psalms into five books. The narrative transcribed from Mark forms the "vertebrae" of the Gospel of Matthew (chapters 3–4, 8–9, 11–12, 14–17, 19–23). Into this arrangement Matthew introduces five blocks of teachings or sayings of Jesus, so placed to serve as commentaries on the unfolding story of Jesus' ministry (chapters 5–7, 10, 13, 18, and 24–25). As the outline clearly reveals, in each book Matthew recounts a sequence of events in the ministry of Jesus, followed by a collection of sayings, parables, or instructions appropriate to what is happening in Jesus' own life, and in the life of the first-century church for which Matthew wrote.

The genealogy, preparations for Jesus' coming, and the stories of his birth and infancy introduce the Gospel (chapters 1–2). The Passion narrative and the Resurrection stories conclude the Gospel (chapters 27–28). All the material in the first two chapters is unique to Matthew. (Luke's genealogy differs from Matthew's in significant ways.) The Passion-Resurrection narrative almost certainly circulated among early Christians, first as oral tradition, and perhaps even before Mark's Gospel as a written document.

Against the skyline of Matthew's Gospel a number of towering peaks rise up from which the whole Gospel takes its special meaning. Five in particular provide the distinctive character of this work.

The Christ

At the very beginning announcement is made to Joseph in his dream as to who Jesus is and why he is coming: *You are to give him the name Jesus, because he will save his people from their sins . . . and they will call him Immanuel (which means, God with us)* (NIV, 1:21, 23). Or, as phrased in the NRSV, *you are to name him Jesus, for he will save his people from their sins . . . and they shall call him Emmanuel*

Peter's confession, *You are the Christ* (NIV; NRSV = *Messiah*, 16:16), puts into words the faith out of which Matthew speaks. *Christ* is from the Greek *Christos*, meaning God's anointed or chosen one, sometimes called messiah from the Jewish word for the one who was to rule at the end of the age.

At the end of the episode where Peter fails to walk on the water and Jesus pulls him into the boat, Matthew writes, *And those in the boat worshiped him, saying, "Truly you are the Son of God"* (14:33). The word *worshiped* and the designation *Son of God* convey the understanding of Jesus as the Christ. The same word is used at the very end of the Gospel on the mountain in Galilee when the risen Christ appears to the disciples: *When they saw him they worshiped him* (28:17). The identification of Jesus with the Christ of God puts the authentication of God on everything that Jesus says and does in the Gospel.

Fulfillment

More than any of the other evangelists (Gospel writers), Matthew goes to unceasing lengths to establish that Jesus came to fulfill holy prophecy. Repeatedly we come upon the statement, *This was to fulfil what was spoken through the prophet* . . . (NIV, for example 8:17; 21:4). Matthew brings more than sixty quotations from the Old Testament into his Gospel, anchoring the good news of the coming of the Christ deeply in the soil of Jewish hopes and expectations. Jesus says in the Sermon on the Mount, *I have come not to abolish (the law and the prophets) but to fulfill them* (5:17). A close study of the way Matthew uses Scripture reveals that frequently he bends prophecy to accord with events happening to Jesus. And one strongly suspects that he sometimes bends the report of what takes place in order that it agree with prophecy. One can see this most vividly in 21:2-6, the story of the triumphal entry into Jerusalem, where the story seems to have Jesus riding *two* beasts into the Holy City because the prophecy appears that way in Zechariah 9:9. But whatever distortions may lie in Matthew's use of the Old Testament, the effect of his vision is to weave an unbreakable strand around Jesus and his Jewish predecessors, biding them in faith, hope, and covenant.

Apocalyptic

The stress which the evangelist puts on the apocalyptic Christ is unmistakable. Apocalyptic faith believes that at the heavenly-appointed time God will overthrow the ruler of this present age of darkness and evil and establish the eternal rule of blessedness. Matthew identifies Jesus the Christ with this figure of Jewish apocalyptic expectation. With Matthew the center of history lies in the future, at the day of judgment, of which Matthew gives us glimpses in Chapters 24–25. Throughout the Gospel are recurring references to *darkness*, where *there will be weeping and gnashing of teeth* (25:30). The heavy news of Matthew's Gospel to the church for which it was written was that the apocalypse is coming soon. Said John the Baptist, *Even now the ax is lying at the root of the trees* (NRSV, 3:10).

The Church

Apocalyptic emphasis notwithstanding, Matthew shows no less concern for the church, an institution within which people must be disciplined to live *now*. Matthew leaves no doubt that Jesus the risen Lord is present in the community of believers. At the heart of the chapter on church discipline and administration Jesus promises in Chapter 18, verse 20, *Where two or three are gathered in my name, I am there among them* (NRSV). *Where two or three come together in my name, there am I with them* (NIV). At his final appearance to his disciples Jesus promises to those who have taken up God's mission, *I am with you to the end of the age* (28:20). Matthew is the only one of the four evangelists to use the Greek word *ekklesia*, meaning *church*—a people who are called out of society to a life in covenant with each other and with their risen Lord. In fact, Chapter 18 is a manual of discipline for church members who were living between the appearing of Christ and the day of judgment.

Ethical Righteousness

The Gospel of Matthew might well be called a summons to righteousness. Among the Beatitudes is this blessing, *Blessed are those who hunger and thirst for righteousness* (5:6), and the more explicit, *Blessed are those who are persecuted for righteousness' sake* (5:10 NRSV; NIV = *because of righteousness*). Later in the Sermon on the Mount Jesus commands, *Seek first his kingdom and his righteousness* (NIV, 6:33). Righteousness means being faithful to the covenant that binds the church (the new Israel) to God. It means being right with God. Throughout the Gospel Matthew stresses the importance of ethical obedience to the higher righteousness (5:20). It was to fulfill *all* righteousness that Jesus was baptized (3:15).

Setting

We do not know who wrote (compiled) this Gospel. It is improbable that Matthew the tax collector and disciple could be the author, although his memories could be scattered through these pages. Of some things we may be sure. This Gospel is the work of a Jewish Christian, one who brings the faith and traditions of Israel to the new covenant. The book was prepared for a congregation (or congregations) of Jewish Christians in a time of controversy between the followers of Christ and the Jewish priestly establishment of the late first century. Sometime between the fall of Jerusalem (to the Romans in A.D. 70) and the end of the century Christians were expelled from the synagogues. The intensity of the conflict between Jesus and the scribes and Pharisees, apparent in this gospel, may indeed reflect the conflict between Jews and Christians in the bitter years between 70 and 100. Apocalyptic fervor was strong in northern Palestine. This invites the speculation that Matthew may have been written for Christians in one or more of the cities of Syria. One cannot be more precise as to date and location. What is beyond any question is that this Gospel comes out of the crucible of the first century when the followers of Christ faced both persecution and apocalyptic judgment. The Gospel prepared for them has not ceased to be good news for us, their descendants in the crucible of the twentieth century.

Matthew 1–2

Introduction to These Chapters

Chapters 1 and 2 form a prelude to the Gospel of
Matthew. Like a prelude or overture to a music drama,
the principal themes we will hear throughout the drama
are sounded in clear statement. Before the curtain even
rises on the life of Jesus the evangelist gives an
announcement of what the Gospel is all about: *Jesus the
Christ, Emmanuel of God, has come in fulfillment of the
promises God made to Israel, beginning with Abraham. He
comes not only as the royal heir of David but with salvation
for the whole world.* These are the ruling themes of
Matthew's Gospel. The evangelist heralds these themes
by means of a genealogy, a divine annunciation of the
holy birth, the story of Jesus' birth, attended by a
heavenly epiphany, the appearing of wise men from
beyond Israel to worship, and by God's special
providence for him who is to be the *Son of the living God*
(16:16).

Here is an outline of these chapters.
  I. Genealogy (1:1-17)
  II. Annunciation and Conception (1:18-25)
  III. The Birth of Jesus (2:1-12)
  IV. Flight Into Egypt and Return (2:13-23)

Genealogy (1:1-17)

Genealogy means *genesis* (1:1). These are the origins, the
beginnings of the work God will perform through Jesus.

Jesus Christ (1:1) is used here, although nowhere else in the Gospel, as a full name. By the time of this Gospel it may have become common to speak of Jesus in this way. But Christ is not really a surname; rather it is a title (as in 1:18) for the anointed one, the Messiah.

Matthew divides the forty-two names into three clusters of fourteen names each. People have long wondered why Matthew chose the equation three times fourteen equals forty-two. Numerology was important to the Hebrews; two, three, and seven were significant numbers. Fourteen may also be a Hebrew symbol for David. In any case the line from Abraham (1:2) to David (1:6) links Jesus with the primary patriarch of Israel, and with the king whose descendant will be the promised Messiah.

The span from David to the time of deportation (1:11) identifies Jesus with the bitter sorrow of Israel's shame, humiliation, and reconciliation with God. The final group of fourteen names comes down to Jesus' own birth to Mary.

Notice that four women are mentioned (three by name), most unusual for a patriarchal society. Tamar (1:3) committed adultery (Genesis 38); Rahab (1:5) was a harlot in Jericho (Joshua 2:1-7); Ruth (1:5) was an alien (Ruth 1:4); Uriah's wife was partner with David in adultery (2 Samuel 11 and 12). Matthew seems to say by this inclusion that sinners participated in the lineage that led to the one who knew no sin. Some names that appear in the Old Testament succession of kings Matthew leaves out of his list. Nevertheless, unbroken continuity binds Jesus with the heritage of Israel.

The genealogy calls Joseph *the husband of Mary* (1:16), not the father of Jesus. Thus it does not compromise the virgin birth (1:18). But in this genealogy the blood ancestry comes as far as Joseph, then does not pass through to Jesus. One cannot logically trace ancestry through the male line as Israel did, and still accept birth from a virgin mother. The tradition upon which Matthew draws takes no account of such an inconsistency. Everything about this birth was surprising; Jesus' birth to a woman not in the Davidic ancestral line (as far as we know) was part of the whole mystery. But the mystery can be wrapped around by the faith that God who *is able from these stones to raise up children to (for) Abraham* (3:9) can leap the genetic gap between Joseph and Jesus.

The Annunciation and Conception (1:18-25)

In Luke's Gospel the annunciation of the birth of Jesus comes to Mary from the angel Gabriel (Luke 1:26-38). The annunciation in Matthew comes to Joseph in a dream (1:20). Five times in these two chapters people were guided by their dreams (1:20; 2:12; 2:13; 2:19; 2:22). In those days people trusted the messages, warnings, and revelations that appeared in dreams; dreams were accepted as a way in which God communicated with people. Recall the dreams of Jacob (Genesis 28) and Pharaoh (Genesis 41). The mechanism of how this took place did not trouble those who transmitted the tradition. They saw in dreams the device by which awareness and warning were seen and heard. Through the dreams of Joseph and the wise men (1:20 and 2:12) God protected and provided for the Holy Child.

Mary had been engaged (NRSV; NIV = *pledged to be married to Joseph*, 1:18). Betrothal was far more binding at that time, and in that society, than engagement is today. In every way except the marriage bed Joseph and Mary were bound by marital pledge and covenant. When Joseph would later take Mary to his home and consummate their union, they would be fully husband and wife. But during betrothal, when conception occurred, every obligation and fidelity of the covenant was expected. So when Mary found herself pregnant, it could only mean adultery and scandal. Not wanting to put Mary to this public shame, Joseph resolved to divorce her quietly.

In the economy of God Joseph had to be the instrument to protect this unborn child. To that end God revealed who and what Jesus would become (1:21-23). The compelling truth to which this announcement bears witness is one that early Christians needed and welcomed: *Jesus was a child of God's Holy Spirit.* What appeared at first to be scandal turned out to be the way of God's incarnation in Jesus. Greater become the surprises of Jesus' nativity. The miracle of the virgin birth is a tradition pointing to the supreme miracle of the incarnation of God in Jesus the Christ. Other than Matthew and Luke the New Testament is silent about Jesus' conception. Apparently to Mark, to John, and to Paul the tradition of the virgin birth was not a matter essential to Christian faith.

The Birth of Jesus (2:1-12)

As a remarkable cameo of literature, and as the enduring inspiration for much art and music, this simple account of the birth of Jesus has remained a favorite story among Christians from the beginning. It holds a high place as well for what it tells us about Jesus and what his coming was to mean to the world.

From this story (as from Luke's nativity account) we learn the tradition that Jesus was born in Bethlehem during the reign of Herod the Great (2:1). Herod had been installed as the Roman puppet king of the Jews in 40 B.C., a throne he occupied until his death in 4 B.C. Although he was not a Jew himself, Herod's third wife Mariamne was of Jewish royalty. We shall look more closely at the frightful Herodian family further along in Jesus' life when he encountered them for himself (chapter 14). To King Herod came the wise men from the East. The Gospel does not call them "kings" as we sing in the Christmas hymn, nor does it give them names. They were probably astrologers from Persia, men who studied the heavens for signs portending important events on earth.

We serve little purpose in seeking for some naturalistic explanation of the star they followed (2:2). The Gospel does not explain the star. Rather the story has as its purpose to reveal that the birth of Jesus was a divine intervention of God in the life of Israel. That intervention was signaled by a heavenly epiphany, not just for Israel but for the world beyond as well. These wise men were from another country, yet Jesus inspired their worship (2:11). One naturally thinks in this connection of the prophecies in Isaiah: *And nations shall come to your light, and kings to the brightness of your rising (dawn) . . . They shall bring gold and frankincense (incense)* (Isaiah 60:3, 6). Isaiah spoke in prophecy about Israel. For the Christian, Jesus inaugurated the new Israel.

The story tells us they *came to a house* (2:11). There is nothing here about an inn or a stable (as in Luke). But the two traditions about Jesus' birth are independent, and in no need of reconciliation. They both herald the good news in quite different settings. People have speculated that the visit of the wise men may have come some time later than the adoration of the shepherds on the night when Jesus was born, perhaps as much as two years later if Herod set out to kill all children in Bethlehem of two years and younger (2:16). It has also been surmised that in Matthew's Gospel Joseph and his family were living in Bethlehem, whereas in Luke the holy family were transients from Nazareth, in Bethlehem only because of the Roman enrollment. Matthew, of course, had in view the prophecy spoken by Micah (2:5-6), a detail with which Luke had no concern. The word *house* may be a mistranslation of the word *inside* (2:11).

Once again a dream becomes the instrument to account for what happens to Jesus. Because of their dream the wise men chose not to return to Herod on their way back to their own country. It would hardly be surprising if their dream confirmed an intuition of Herod's malevolence aroused by their meeting with the king in Jerusalem. The confrontation between Herod and the wise men almost certainly stands as a metaphor for the way Jesus, and later the Christian church, will have to contend with powerful establishments, first of all the rulers in Israel. Here we see the contrast and the sharp lines drawn between the hostility of the powerful, represented by King Herod, and the receptivity of the Gentiles, seen in the wise men, a contrast we shall see often as Matthew recounts the ministry of Jesus. (For examples see 4:15-16 and 15:21-28.)

Flight into Egypt and Return (2:13-23)

This episode of danger and escape begins with another dream in which the Lord warns Joseph to flee the wrath of Herod by escaping to Egypt (2:13). Like all autocrats, Herod feared any pretender to his power. But why Egypt? In order to fulfill what God had said through the prophet, *Out of Egypt I called my son* (Hosea 11:1). Here we see again Matthew's appeal to fulfillment of Scripture. When we turn to Hosea, however, we discover that what the prophet was talking about was God's deliverance of Israel in the Exodus, far back in her history, not a prediction to be later fulfilled by the messiah. While it is true that Matthew wants to identify every possible place where the events of Jesus' life fulfill prophecy, in this case there is more to it than that. It had become important for Jewish Christians in the apostolic period to see in Jesus the recapitulation of Israel's history. Deliverance from Egypt was the definitive event in their national life. Now they would see Jesus the Christ as a new Moses, bringing his followers out of another Egypt. Thus Matthew's appeal to this Scripture has a symbolic validity much deeper than the mere repetition of a physical journey. So the flight into Egypt was escape from Herod on the one hand, but it also prepared for the re-enactment of the Exodus.

Compared to the Holocaust, or other instances of genocide that have disgraced our history, the killing of a few children in Bethlehem seems like a minor incident in this world of violence. But the import of the Gospel is that wherever a single innocent child is murdered there is moral outrage. The brutality of this monster Herod cannot be measured in numbers.

Jeremiah's image of Rachel weeping for her children (Jeremiah 31:15) takes us back to the deportation of the Israelites to Babylon in 597 B.C. The prophet, seeing the grief of the departing exiles, remembers how Jacob (Israel) refused to be comforted at the supposed death of his son Joseph (Genesis 37:35). Matthew sees another occasion for grief that cannot be assuaged.

Now Herod finally dies, and Joseph (in Egypt) is called in a dream to return to Israel. But Archelaeus, as brutish and fearful as his father, has come to power in Judea. This man will later murder a whole gathering of Jews in the Temple at Passover. Once more the Lord speaks to Joseph in a dream, telling him to go to Galilee. Down through the years this childhood event will have significance. Galilee would become the scene of Jesus' greatest popularity, whereas opposition leading to his death would be centered in Jerusalem.

Why Nazareth? The text is not clear in calling Jesus a Nazarene. Nazareth is not mentioned in any Old Testament prophecy. The word *Nazarene* derives from *nazir,* meaning *root* or *stump,* in which case it could well refer to the prophecy: *A shoot will come up from the stump of Jesse* (NIV, Isaiah 11:1).

§ § § § § § §

The Message of Matthew 1–2

Chapters 1 and 2 of Matthew's Gospel do more than just prepare for what follows. The prelude itself announces good news. This above all: In a world often inhospitable to our hopes and dreams, where we feel frightened and lonely here and now, and threatened by what may happen in the future, in this world *God is with us.* Jesus the Christ comes even yet *to forgive people the sins that burden their lives.* To the familiar question, "What's in a name?" Matthew answers: In the name of Jesus is God's presence and God's forgiveness.

The birth story speaks to our imagination in two ways. The wise men can be examples for us. They made a long and perilous journey to come to the Christ, following a strange and unfamiliar star. So must be many human journeys to the Christ. The question they asked upon arriving in Jerusalem is a universal one: "Where is he who has been born . . . ?" We identify with them in asking, Where will we find the one with power to save?

Dark shadows also fall upon these pages, peopled with those who *sought the young child's life.* The shadows did not flee away when Herod and Archelaeus vanished from the scene. Sometimes the message of the Gospel comes in the form of questions we are compelled to answer. Little children remain vulnerable to the world's evil; what sanctuaries can we find to which they may be taken for safety? How disturbing, if we are honest with ourselves, to realize that most human beings are strange compounds of both Joseph and Herod. The Gospel is asking, How is it with us?

§ § § § § § §

MATTHEW

Matthew 3–4

Introduction to These Chapters

With chapter 3 Matthew begins the first of five so-called books into which he divides his Gospel. Chapters 3 and 4 contain the narrative account of the beginning of Jesus' ministry; chapters 5 through 7 include the teaching discourse on discipleship, what we call the Sermon on the Mount.

Here is an outline of chapters 3–4.

I. Preaching of John the Baptist (3:1-4)
II. Crowds Are Baptized (3:5-6)
III. Challenge to the Pharisees and Sadducees (3:7-10)
IV. John's Announcement (3:11-12)
V. Jesus Is Baptized (3:13-17)
VI. Jesus' Temptation (4:1-11)
VII. John's Arrest (4:12-16)
VIII. Jesus Comes Preaching (4:17)
IX. Jesus Calls His First Disciples (4:18-22)
X. Teaching, Preaching, and Healing (4:23-25)

Preaching of John the Baptist (3:1-4)

It had been a long time since a prophet had appeared in Israel. Now at last one came who followed in the great tradition of speaking to the nation for God. Several things about John stirred the people to an uncommon degree. First, his message: *The kingdom of heaven has come near* (NRSV). This was the apocalyptic announcement for which many in Israel had long waited. *Kingdom of heaven*

21

means the kingly rule of God; to say that such a rule was near meant that the end time of apocalyptic hope was approaching.

Jewish hope anticipated that before the messiah came Elijah would appear. Seeing John wearing camel's hair and a leather girdle, people thought of the ancient prophecy written in 2 Kings 1:8. More than that, they saw him preparing the way of the Lord in the wilderness, as the prophet had declared this forerunner would do (Isaiah 40:3). For the prophet, "the way" meant a "highway for our God"; to Matthew "the Lord" meant Jesus, the Christ. To the imminent fulfillment of apocalyptic hope, the reappearance of one like Elijah, and the making of a path for the Lord, people fervently responded.

Crowds Are Baptized (3:5-6)

It was highly unusual for faithful Jews to be baptized. Proselyte baptism of new converts they did practice, and ritual washing to remove uncleanness was part of Jewish liturgical life. But hardly mass baptism for repentance and the confession of sins. One may infer from this practice that John thought of Israel being so far gone in corruption that the whole people needed to confess their sins and signal repentance by turning their lives around; repent means to "turn around" toward God. John called for a radical redirection of life.

Challenge to the Pharisees and Sadducees (3:7-10)

In John's confrontation with Pharisees and Sadducees we meet for the first time the adversaries who will plague Jesus all the way to the cross, especially the Pharisees. Pharisee meant literally "to be separated." They were the party in Israel who separated themselves from all who were careless, from all who neglected the matters of cleanliness, diet, and obedience to the hundreds of ritual requirements of Jewish law. They were devoted to purity and fidelity toward the law. Being a faithful Jew in the midst of pagan culture was both demanding and dangerous. The Pharisees held high the law in a time of religious compromise. But the dark side of their strict adherence to obedience was a self-righteousness and a hardness of heart to all who failed to measure up.

The Sadducees were a conservative priestly group, entrenched in power and clinging tightly to established ways and institutions. Both Pharisees and Sadducees were threatened by any popular movement centered on a leader like John the Baptist. They feared him as a danger to the status quo.

John perceived their insincerity in coming to be baptized. He knew they would not truly repent when they went into the water, nor would they confess their sins. The only repentance-baptism acceptable was one that bore the fruits of ethical righteousness. Not words, or ritual acts, but deeds. Worst of all, the Pharisees and Sadducees justified themselves because they were sons of Abraham. To this plea John gave sharp answer (3:9). Jesus was to echo this rejoinder in his own teaching: *Not everyone who says to me, "Lord, Lord," will enter the kingdom of heaven, but only the one who does the will of my Father* (NRSV, Matthew 7:21). And as to sons of Abraham: *The tax collectors and the prostitutes are entering the kingdom of God before you* (NIV, 21:31).

John's Announcement (3:11-12)

Fire may have been the only baptism heralded by John. When the messiah comes, the unrepentant will be consumed in judgment. They will be like chaff *burned with unquenchable fire.* When this Gospel was written for the apostolic church, the words about baptism by the Holy Spirit may have been added following Pentecost, where Peter quoted so much of Joel's prophecy about the Spirit (Joel 2:28-32; Acts 2:17-21).

Jesus Is Baptized (3:13-17)

This episode breaks into three parts: the exchange between John and Jesus (verses 13-14); the baptism itself (verse 15); and the manifestation to Jesus and to the observers as Jesus came up from the river (verses 16-17).

In Matthew's Gospel John recognized who Jesus was and felt inadequate to baptize God's "beloved Son." From the earliest days the Christian church has needed to explain why Jesus the Christ submitted to a baptism of repentance, confessing his sins. According to the tradition from which this exchange is drawn, John's protest to Jesus gave Jesus the occasion to address the question: *It is proper for us to fulfill all righteousness,* meaning "to fulfill every religious duty." Since righteousness is one of the principal themes of Matthew's Gospel, it is important to associate Jesus with "all righteousness" from the very beginning. If Jesus is to save his people from their sins, he will identify with them in performing their religious duty.

We can also read the verses as an account of the anointing of Jesus for his ministry. John, the forerunner, in effect "ordained" Jesus, as they collaborated in fulfilling the prophecies of Isaiah of the Exile (Isaiah 40:3; 42:1). The Spirit enabled Jesus to do the messiah's work. One of Matthew's ruling purposes is to declare Jesus as the Christ, God's chosen one. Verses 16-17 become critically important to that intention: *This is my Son. . . .*

But how do we understand the event as Matthew describes it? Apparently Jesus alone saw the Spirit of God descending like a dove. Did Jesus later report this to others? But when the *voice from heaven* spoke, it was to the crowds. In Mark's version the whole event was private to Jesus alone (Mark 1:9-11).

The *dove* is the symbol of God's Spirit, which was to be with Jesus from that time forth. The words of anointing are from Psalm 2:7, one of the psalms used at the coronation of kings in Israel, and from Isaiah 42:1, the anointing of the servant of the Lord. Two central traditions in the hope of Israel came together at the baptism of Jesus: a messiah, who was a son of David, and a suffering servant of the Lord. Their coming together in the person of Jesus is an important factor in the struggle reflected throughout the Gospel of Matthew between the early followers of Jesus and the authorities in Israel— between church and synagogue.

Jesus' Temptation (4:1-11)

The key to understanding why God's Spirit should lead Jesus to be tempted by the devil lies in the word *temptation*. This is not an enticement or seduction to do evil, as we customarily use the word, but a *testing*, a *trial* of his fidelity. Immediately when Jesus was baptized, or anointed for his ministry, he had to be tested to see if he was capable of faithful obedience. The devil is sometimes called *Satan* in the New Testament (Mark 1:13). Satan is the lord of the kingdom of evil, at war with the power of God. The battle in this Judean wilderness was fought for high stakes within the soul of Jesus—the soul of him who had just been called God's beloved Son.

The first test was to see how Jesus would use the power of the Spirit that had been given to him: for material things or for the word of God. Jesus' answer does not imply that we need no bread. Rather Jesus is called to speak God's word, which is a word about more than bread.

The second test was to see if he would perform some sign affording proof of God's faithfulness. In his answer Jesus offered not proof or signs, but faith. One cannot put God to the test.

The third test (in Luke's Gospel, the second; see Luke 4:5-8) was for Jesus to conquer the kingdoms of the world by worshiping the devil. In his dismissal of Satan Jesus appealed to the first commandment (Deuteronomy 5:7). Satan offered a shortcut based on the deception that the ends justify the means. Jesus refused the tempting offer, choosing rather the way of suffering love.

The temptations were really a trial to show what kind of messiah Jesus would be. Through the temptations he demonstrated that the devil would not call the tune of his ministry, and that he would submit only to God's Spirit (4:4). He also refused to put God to the test (4:7), and he chose not to compromise in those days whom he would serve.

John's Arrest (4:12-16)

Matthew is silent about what Jesus may have done following his testing in the wilderness. But when Herod arrested John, Jesus suddenly appeared. With the moral outrage of Herod's injustice, the tide in the affairs of Israel reached a flood. Jesus launched his ministry on that flood.

He commenced his work in Galilee, a region heavily populated by Gentiles. It was to the non-Jews that the apostles later preached the gospel. It must have seemed fitting to Matthew that Jesus began his ministry in "Galilee of the Gentiles." The territories of Zebulun and Naphtali lay west of the Sea of Galilee; through them ran two great international highways. Nowhere but in Jerusalem itself could the ministry of Jesus have attracted more important attention. And Jesus was not yet ready for the opposition centered in Jerusalem. Matthew saw the place of the inauguration of Jesus' ministry as fulfillment of Isaiah 9:1-2.

Jesus Comes Preaching (4:17)

Jesus began his preaching by repeating John's message, *Repent for the kingdom of heaven has come near* (NRSV). That God's rule was very near, fulfilled the ancient expectation. Later Jesus would elaborate this announcement to his disciples (chapters 13 and 25). Here he heralded the news to everyone in the form of a *proclamation* ("The kingdom of heaven is near") and a *prescription* ("Repent").

Jesus Calls His First Disciples (4:18-22)

Even as he spoke, Jesus looked beyond the first announcement. The gospel of the Kingdom would need interpreters, teachers, and ambassadors, *in Jerusalem and in all Judea and Samaria and to the ends of the earth* (Acts 1:8). Without delay he began to gather disciples (literally *learners*, ones who would follow a teacher or a doctrine).

Peter and Andrew, James and John would continue as the core of the disciples. Much has been made of how these two sets of brothers immediately dropped their nets, turned away from their families, and went on with Jesus. They may already have known Jesus (see John 1:35-42). This is not the crux of the matter, however. When Jesus invited these fishermen to join him in his work they made his work first in their lives. Matthew could hardly mean that every follower of Christ was to abandon all other responsibility. Jesus' work would be done in a thousand ways, in ten thousand places.

Teaching, Preaching, and Healing (4:23-25)

Jesus taught in the synagogues, preached to the crowds, and healed every disease and infirmity. This was the work of ministry, a preview of the gospel to follow. Mostly it was work among the Jews, but the report that his fame had spread to all Syria and the Decapolis, largely inhabited by Greeks, means that his influence already extended beyond Israel. If the Gospel of Matthew was written for a church, or churches, in Syria, this reference would have been received with interest.

Disease in that day was attributed to demon possession. Verse 24 shows the power Jesus was to display again and again throughout Matthew's Gospel.

§ § § § § § §

The Message of Matthew 3–4

Both John the Baptist and Jesus began their ministry preaching "Repent, for the kingdom of heaven is at hand." The message is both proclamation and prescription. There is a maxim by which authentic Christian preaching can be identified: *The imperative is in the indicative.* In other words, because God has sent Jesus the Christ among us to be the way, the truth, and the life (indicative), we ought to turn around and follow him (imperative). Repentance is not only necessary, but possible, *on account of what God has done.*

In John's indictment of the Pharisees and Sadducees we would not expect to find much of a word for Christians today. The setting and the dynamics seem poles apart. But by our very assumption that we are not like the Pharisees, do we not give ourselves away? Sometimes we think we have the best family ties, we keep the commandments, we are members of the church in good standing, and we pray faithfully. Put all that boasting together and it comes out sounding like, "We have Abraham as our Father." Self-righteousness may be the most dangerous of sins; it blinds us to our real need of a new heart.

We live in an age that understands and responds to endorsements. Advertisers know the value of finding a "big name" to endorse the products they sell. Matthew knew how important it was that Jesus the Christ have unquestioned credentials. None could appeal to a higher credential than a voice from heaven saying, "You are my beloved Son." The truth to which that voice bore witness remains for us today.

§ § § § § § §

PART THREE

Matthew 5–7

Introduction to These Chapters

Chapters 5–7 form the teaching discourse in Matthew's first section. This section has come to be known as the Sermon on the Mount, so called because Matthew places the setting for this discourse on a mountain. Whether it was to parallel Moses receiving the law on Mount Sinai is something on which scholars do not agree. Luke 6:17-49 includes some, but not all, of the material in Matthew 5–7. Luke puts the sermon *on a level place,* giving rise to the name, the Sermon on the Plain. In Luke Jesus addresses a great multitude. In Matthew he speaks to the disciples alone.

These three chapters constitute the most systematic arrangement of what discipleship means. This is what the disciples are to teach those who become followers of Jesus. The evangelist places it here immediately following the call of Jesus' first disciples (4:18-22) and the summary of how he went about Galilee teaching in the synagogues (4:23). This is not a "sermon" in the sense we think of sermons, preached from a pulpit in a worship service. It is a summary of what disciples/teachers are to teach and what believers are to do.

Here is an outline of chapters 5–7.

I. The Beatitudes (5:3-12)
II. Disciples as Salt and Light (5:13-16)
III. Jesus and the Law (5:17-20)
IV. "You Have Heard . . . " (5:21-48)

The Beatitudes (5:3-12)

A beatitude is a blessing. "How happy!" in God's sight are those to whom Jesus refers—the poor in spirit, the mourners, the meek, and the others.

Those who mourn (verse 4) are those who grieve for the sins and sorrows of the world. God will console them in the new age.

Blessed are the meek (verse 5) has been called Jesus' incredible beatitude. The beatitude does not take the usual sense of our word *meek.* It signifies not weakness, but one who is aware of his or her own limitations. Because they have this awareness, the meek know how much they must depend on God.

Instead of Luke's single word *hunger* (Luke 6:21), Matthew includes *and thirst for righteousness* (verse 6), making it a blessing for all who yearn for an upright life. Those who seek goodness with all their hearts will be satisfied in the time of God's promised rule.

Only those who show *mercy* to others can receive God's mercy (verse 7), because divine mercy cannot enter a heart that is not itself merciful.

The *pure in heart* (verse 8) are not the morally perfect. They are the ones who seek above all else to come before God. You will find God if you search with all your heart (see Deuteronomy 4:29).

Peace in the biblical sense is more than just the absence of conflict. It is harmony and well-being, both within oneself and among all people. Because these qualities are what God wants for all creation, we become true sons and daughters of God when we strive for peace (verse 9).

The ancient Jewish word *shalom* (peace), used 172 times in the Old Testament, has no single English equivalent that captures its full meaning.

The kingdom of heaven belongs to those who have suffered for the sake of God's righteousness (verse 10).

In verse 11 Jesus speaks in direct address to the disciples. They *will be* persecuted because they are loyal to him, and disciples are not above their master. But they are to rejoice, because in the kingdom of heaven they will find blessing.

The Beatitudes are instructions in how to live the Christian life. They are also promises about the kingdom of heaven, both now and in the age to come. While there is much universal wisdom and morality in the Beatitudes, their full meaning comes only from the gospel (good news) of the Christ, God with us. (See "The Message of Matthew 5–7.")

Disciples as Salt and Light (5:13-16)

In an age when people have become conscious of how too much salt is harmful to health, it may be difficult to appreciate the importance of salt in Jesus' day. Salt preserved food and gave it flavor. In the same way, the followers of the Christ would preserve the world and give life its true taste. The disciples are also to be a light in the world's darkness. They will be tempted to hide the light of Christ when threatened by those who hate the light. As the two similes stand, we can read them as sayings to the church. When salt grows insipid and light is extinguished, they henceforth become useless.

Jesus and the Law (5:17-20)

These verses about Jesus and the law seem inconsistent with many other things Jesus said and did. For example, *Not the smallest letter . . . will disappear from the law* (NIV) is hardly consistent with Matthew 12:1-6, the episode where the disciples pluck grain on the sabbath and Jesus justifies such an infraction of the law. By these four axioms (5:17-20) Matthew would meet the accusation that Jesus sweeps away the law, which is the foundation of Israel. The six antitheses (5:21-48) we can read as interpretations of what Jesus means by fulfillment of the law.

"You Have Heard . . . " (5:21-48)

The first two antitheses between the old laws and the new commandments (5:21-23) do not imply that the law be suspended. Rather, the issue should be met on the inner ground of moral intention. This is an example of the righteousness of the disciples exceeding that of the Pharisees (5:20).

The remaining four antitheses (5:31-48) imply laws to be superseded by new commandments.

It is still morally indefensible to murder, but Jesus drives the issue inward to the anger, contempt, and hatred, which lead a person to murder (verses 21-26). Many Jews believed in "the hell of fire" where sinners were punished after death.

Adultery is prohibited as always. But lust, which precedes adultery, is no less immoral than the act itself (5:27-30). In these verses Jesus speaks in characteristic hyperbole—exaggerating in the extreme to call for purity of attitude.

Mark (10:11-12) and Luke (16:18) report Jesus saying that anyone who divorces his wife and marries another commits adultery. Matthew qualifies the unequivocal law by allowing *the ground of unchastity* NRSV; NIV = *marital unfaithfulness* (verse 32). In either case the old law (Deuteronomy 24:1-4) is superseded. (For a further discussion of marriage and divorce see Matthew 19:3-9.)

Jesus dismisses the whole practice of oaths. Disciples are to tell the truth under all circumstances. Why should we need oaths? In this we have an illustration of why the Sermon on the Mount is not a code applicable in society as a whole, but only to Christians who have heard and

MATTHEW

believe the gospel. Oaths in our judicial system provide a sanction where people may not honor the truth.

Do not resist an evildoer (NRSV; NIV = *evil person*, verse 39) contradicts the ancient law (Exodus 21:23-25) of *an eye for an eye.* Jesus rejects the whole idea of retaliation; disciples are to respond by grace rather than revenge. For this attitude Christian disciples were often struck on the right cheek, as were heretics.

Love your enemies and pray for those who persecute you (verse 44) is the way God loves, not as self-serving tax collectors and sinners love. Jews particularly despised those who served their Roman overlords by collecting their taxes, especially when the collectors were Jews themselves (verse 46). *Agape* is the word Matthew uses in this passage. We may translate it as *good will,* seeking only the best for the ones who are loved. Love is not so much a feeling in the heart as a resolution in the mind to actively seek goodness for neighbors and enemies alike.

Perfect (verse 48) does not mean moral perfection. The Greek word is *teleios,* meaning *ended* or *complete.* We are to be like God in our *intentions,* in the purposes of love and mercy, which we serve. In so doing we *complete* the purpose for which God created us.

Practicing Piety (6:1-18)

The three illustrations that Jesus chooses from the practice of Jewish piety contrast the difference between practicing piety to win the praises of people and true devotion to God practiced in secret. The contrasts have to do with motive. The structure is memorable. Each of the three stanzas begins with the formula: *When you . . .* (6:2, 5, 16), then moves to a comparison with the hypocrites, and how to practice devotion privately, concluding with *your Father who sees what is done in secret* (6:4, 6, 18).

When You Give Alms (6:2-4)

Giving money out of pity for the relief of the poor was an essential part of faithful devotion among the Jews. By

Matthew's time this practice had passed on to the Christian church. Sounding a trumpet called public attention to the act of almsgiving so everyone would know of the giver's generosity. *Hypocrites* means literally, *play actors.* To give as a play actor, pretending to a piety one does not have, robs the act of its sincerity.

When You Pray (6:5-8)

It was customary to stand for prayer. The hypocrites loved to do it in the most conspicuous places. In verse 7, *empty phrases* (NRSV) means, in Greek, *to babble* which is used in the NIV translation of this verse. Babbling does not impress God.

The Lord's Prayer (6:9-15)

Luke's version (11:2-4) is probably closer to the original text. Matthew has adapted the prayer to liturgical use, adding the doxology at the end (a marginal reading in the NIV and NRSV).

The prayer contains seven petitions, the first three (verses 9-10) concerned with God's name, God's kingdom, and God's will. The final four (verses 11-13) are concerned with human needs: daily bread, forgiveness, temptation, and deliverance from evil. Matthew has probably inserted the prayer into Jesus' discourse at this point because it related to the practice of piety.

The first three petitions are really a prayer for the coming of God's kingdom, for the day of universal practice on earth of God's holy will.

We are to ask God for our necessities each day (some translations have it "for the morrow"). This may be seen as a contrast to the acquisitive accumulation of provisions for much time to come.

The petition for forgiveness is contingent upon the petitioners' having forgiven those who sinned against them.

The word translated *temptation* here refers to the terrible time of testing at the end time of apocalyptic hope, "the birth pangs of the Messiah." We should not assume that God would ever lead a person deliberately into temptation to sin.

The final petition may be a prayer to be saved from the Evil One (Satan).

When You Fast (6:16-18)

Like almsgiving and prayer, Jesus warns against fasting so that people will notice. Fasting should not be occasion for ostentation in public but piety in private.

Treasures in Heaven (6:19-21)

Jesus warns against accumulating treasures that are consumed, that wear out or can be stolen. If these become our treasures, these our hearts will worship. Treasures in heaven are the blessings Jesus has promised to all who await God's kingdom in the faith (see, for example, the Beatitudes).

The Sound Eye (6:22-23)

If your eye is sound (healthy, generous), your life will be illumined by God's truth. If your eye is not sound (ungenerous, grudging), your soul will be dark. This analogy follows naturally the saying about treasures, for in the dark we care more for "treasures on earth."

Serving Two Masters (6:24)

One cannot be a slave of his or her wealth and at the same time a devoted servant of God, because one can never belong to two masters. *Mammon*, the original word in the text, is from an Aramaic word (the language Jesus spoke) meaning wealth or money.

Anxiety About Life (6:25-34)

Having just said that no one can serve both God and wealth, Matthew follows with the conjunctive command: *Therefore, do not worry* (verse 25). To worry about life is to be a slave to money. This cycle of verses constitutes one of the unusually hard sayings of Jesus, what seems to us as a kind of impossible counsel of perfection. But we remember that Jesus spoke these words to disciples as he prepared them for their mission in his name. Life would be precarious, they would be penniless, and would suffer persecution "for righteousness' sake." They could not face such a future with sound eye if they were worried.

Jesus' instruction not to worry does not mean what earlier translators rendered, *Take no thought for your life*. We misread Jesus' intention if we consider these words to be an endorsement of improvidence or careless disdain for life. Rather they are a call to exercise faith in God who gave life and who has promised the kingdom of heaven. God will not fail to provide all things needful. This is still a difficult passage for those who lack even the necessities of life. It is a very important passage for those who have what they need, and more, but whose minds and hearts are gripped by anxious worry over keeping it all and getting even more.

Dried grass was used to fuel ovens for baking (verse 30).

Gentiles (NRSV; NIV = *pagans*), people with no faith in the God who promised the kingdom of righteousness, gave way to worry about food, property, and trade.

Do not worry about tomorrow (verse 34) is not a specifically religious proverb, but one whose truth is nevertheless confirmed by all who trust God.

Four Marks of a Disciple (7:1-14)

The first five verses of chapter 7 contain a sharp warning against hard-hearted self-righteousness in judging others. Jesus once again denounces hypocrisy—a charge repeatedly leveled at the synagogue scribes and Pharisees. It is not a prohibition against making moral judgments. The absurd spectacle of a person trying to remove a speck from someone's eye while a log protrudes from his own eye is an example of humor as a weapon of controversy.

The Jews regarded both dogs and swine as unclean animals. The reverence in verse 6 must be to those who show contempt for the disciples' teaching. Such encouragement the disciples needed as they went out to teach in an environment of harsh ridicule. There is a time and place to speak of holy things, not in the pig pen but where the seed can be sown into fertile soil (see 13:1-9).

The twin parables of the loaf and the fish give verses 7-12 a reference to prayer. Verses 7-8 and verse 12 have a broader reference. This is a teaching most pertinent to itinerant disciples traveling without even necessities (see 10:9-11).

Notice the parallelism in verse 7: *Ask . . . seek . . . knock,* and the axiom in the refrain in verse 8: *Everyone who asks . . . every who seeks . . . or everyone who knocks.* The ruling purpose with regard to prayer is to give confidence in God's mercy. The saying in verse 11 has always been troublesome, but John 15:7 helps to anchor it in the unyielding soil of unanswered prayer.

The so-called Golden Rule (7:12) breaks the sequence of verses about prayer. Jesus turns a rabbinical saying from a negative prohibition to a positive command, making it a general rule for behavior. Lifted out of the context of the gift of God's Spirit and the promise of God's kingdom, that is, as a command attached to the gospel, the Golden Rule may be just prudential advice on how to succeed in the world.

The alternative of two ways (verses 13-14) is familiar in Scripture (see Deuteronomy 11:26-29; Joshua 24:15; Jeremiah 21:8). Jesus' words here answer the charges that his way is an easy avoidance of the strict way of the Law and the Prophets.

True and False Teachers (7:15-20)

Verses 15-20 stand as a warning and instruction to the young churches gathered in the name of the Christ (and to all churches since). *Wolves,* which we understand as false teachers, sometimes come in sheep's clothing, with fine credentials. But behind the credentials are hypocrites who repudiate the hard demands of the Kingdom. You will know them by what they *do,* not what they *say.* Jesus then changes the metaphor to one of trees and fruit, an echo of John the Baptist (3:10).

True and False Disciples (7:21-27)

The title "Lord" (verse 21) to early followers of the Christ usually meant their messianic Lord, whose coming would inaugurate the new age. Others might have used the title "Teacher" or "Rabbi." In any case the warning is unmistakable: Just to call Jesus "Lord" will not gain entrance to the Kingdom.

On that day (verse 22) means *when the new day arrives.* Prophecy, exorcism, and mighty works are not enough. Doing *the will of my Father who is in heaven* is the only visa that will admit anyone to the promised blessing.

The contrast between the wise and foolish builders would be familiar to Jesus' hearers. Stream beds in Judea were dry and sandy for most of the year and were easy places in which to build. But in the rainy season the waters roared down to carry away everything in their path. The rain, the floods, and the wind are metaphors for the day of judgment. The parable is eschatological: A time of everlasting consequences draws near.

Summary (7:28-29)

Matthew concludes each of his five "books" with this formula: *And when Jesus had finished saying these things . . .* (11:1; 13:53; 19:1; 26:1).

The scribes taught by appealing to traditional precedent and authority. Jesus' authority was directly from God, within himself. It has been said that with Jesus, teacher and teaching are one.

In Matthew 5:1 Jesus addresses the disciples alone. At the end of this section he seems to be talking to a multitude (*The crowds were astonished* NRSV; NIV = *amazed*). We have no certain way to account for the presence of crowds, unless it was Matthew's way of saying that these teachings were for everyone who would be Jesus' disciples.

§ § § § § § §

The Message of Matthew 5–7

Doing and *being* bring their own blessing. We may be tempted sometimes to think of the Beatitudes (5:3-12) as requirements. If we meet them we will be "rewarded." True, Jesus promises comfort, mercy, inheritance, and satisfaction. But to make these rewards our motives for mourning, mercy, hungering for goodness, and all the others is to miss the nature of God's blessing.

The emphasis of the Sermon on the Mount is on the inner condition of the heart (or soul). It is not enough to refrain from murder and adultery. It is not enough to say prayers, give generously, and participate in religious rituals. It is not enough to say, "Lord, Lord" at the proper time and to do good works. What matters is how we feel in our hearts toward God and our reasons for our behavior.

God's mercy and forgiveness are never measured by our deserving. They are unlimited and unqualified. But it happens that where we have refused or failed to forgive those who have trespassed against us, God's forgiveness cannot reach us (6:14). An unforgiving heart is an effective defense against our own forgiveness.

To worry anxiously betrays a lack of confidence in God (6:25). Our worse fears may be realized tomorrow. But in the long run, as expressed in Deuteronomy 33:27, *The eternal God is your refuge, and underneath are the everlasting arms* (NIV). Moses spoke those words to the people of Israel as they stood on the eve of their entrance into the Promised Land. Jesus speaks the words of 6:25-34 to everyone about to trust the promises of the kingdom of heaven.

To hear Jesus' words and do them (7:24) is to build life securely against washouts and cyclones, to become men and women for all seasons.

§ § § § § § §

Matthew 8–9

Introduction to These Chapters

With chapter 8 Matthew begins the second book of his five-book Gospel. Chapters 8–9 form the narrative portion; chapter 10 contains the teaching discourse on apostleship. Jesus is getting ready to send out his disciples on their mission; the ten incidents of mighty works reported in chapters 8–9 stand as a kind of model or teaching demonstration of what the disciples' healing ministry will be like. The number ten corresponds to the ten wonders performed for the Israelites in Egypt, according to ancient tradition.

The emphasis of these two chapters is on the authority and power of Jesus to heal. The miracles manifest in action the authority with which Jesus spoke in chapters 5–7. One might say these are "credentials" for believing what he taught "on the mountain."

The structure of the narrative is carefully wrought. Ten miracles are reported, in clusters of three, three, and four. Between the first group (8:8-17) and the second (8:28–9:8) we find an interlude (8:18-22) on the requirements for being a disciple. Between the second cluster and the third (9:18-34) Matthew introduces another interlude telling of the calling of Matthew, and the questions which his own disciples and those of John the Baptist asked Jesus.

Here is an outline of chapters 8 and 9.

 I. Three Healings (8:1-17)
 II. Interlude on Discipleship (8:18-22)

III. A Healing and a Mighty Work (8:23-34)
IV. Healing a Paralytic (9:1-8)
 V. Ceremonial Purity and Fasting (9:9-17)
VI. Four Healings (9:18-34)
VII. Summary (9:35-38)

Three Healings (8:1-17)

Many kinds of skin diseases may have been called leprosy. The worst form we can identify as Hansen's disease. With this malady all parts of the body slowly rot away (sometimes over a period as long as thirty years). Lepers were utterly outcast from human society. To touch a leper was not only to risk contagion but made one ceremonially unclean. Jesus transgressed the law in a pointed fashion. After healing the leper he commanded him to obey the requirement of Leviticus 14:2-7 and show himself to the priest. Both Jesus and Matthew knew that Jesus' action would be offensive to the authorities in Israel. So Matthew wanted no suspicion to linger that Jesus acted in contempt of levitical cleansing.

The second incident has an importance for Matthew at three levels. First, we take into account the fact that the centurion was a Gentile, a Roman officer in command of 100 soldiers. Matthew's purpose in reporting the account in detail he reveals in verse 10: *In no one in Israel have I found such faith* (NRSV). The Roman centurion came to Jesus with the faith Jesus expected but failed to find in Israel. In response Jesus said what he would repeat a number of times in the Gospel: *The subjects of the kingdom* (unbelieving Jews) *will be thrown outside, into the darkness* (NIV, 8:12).

The second dimension of this healing is the role of faith in what happened (8:13). Not so much the mighty power of Jesus the wonder worker, but the faith of the centurion made the healing possible. (See "The Message of Matthew 8–9.") The third aspect that arrests attention here is that the healing took place at a distance. Jesus' power is spiritual, not needing the laying on of hands. Jesus' power to heal is not confined to the limit of his physical reach, either in time or distance.

The town of Capernaum was to become Jesus' headquarters for his Galilean ministry, located as it was at the head of the Sea of Galilee. Apparently Capernaum was the home of Peter's wife. Jesus' intervention in the crisis of one of the disciples' families adds a personal and compassionate touch to this chronicle of mighty works. Matthew sees the procession of people coming to Jesus to be healed as fulfillment of Isaiah 53:4, one of the servant passages from Isaiah of the Exile. Later Christians found in this image the prophecy of the suffering servant messiah, taking our sins and infirmities into himself. Matthew here emphasizes the power of the Christ to heal disease.

Interlude on Discipleship (8:18-22)

It is easy to drift over these five familiar verses without a true sense of their disturbing importance. When we read Daniel 7:13-14, we find the image of *one like a son of man* (NIV; NRSV = *one like a human being*) being given dominion, glory, and kingdom. Faithful Jews expected such a messiah coming on the clouds of heaven. But Jesus announces that *the Son of man has nowhere to lay his head* (NRSV, 8:20). Here was an unimagined messiah. With 8:17, 20 Jesus brings together two dimensions of messianic hope in a unique way: suffering and heavenly power.

At first hearing, Jesus' reply to the disciple who wanted to bury his father seems heartless. It is intensely painful, for Jesus is saying in the most unambiguous way that discipleship demands loyalty and commitment beyond all other ties. "Let me go bury my father" was a familiar cop-out, somewhat like saying, "I gave at the office." But the word *dead* can also refer to an old order or covenant. Jesus could be saying here that those who will not go forward to a new covenant can bury the ones who remain behind.

A Healing and a Mighty Work (8:23-34)

Probably because we live in a scientific age, we are apt to focus on the physical, meterological aspects of the calming of the storm. For Matthew the emphasis is on the fear (lack of confidence) of the disciples at the height of the storm and on their marvel and questions that followed in the great calm. We do not know exactly what happened. The account is clear that the disciples were full of fear. This augured poorly for the mission upon which they were soon to embark. Jesus' question (8:26) goes to the heart of the matter: Have you no confidence in God, who is Lord of winds and waves?

Mark's gospel (Mark 5:1-20) gives us a much longer and more detailed picture of the encounter with the two demoniacs among the tombs in the country beyond the Sea of Galilee. Reflected in these accounts is the conviction that such a disturbed person, screaming and raving, hurting himself and breaking every restraint, was possessed by demons. It was universally accepted that what we would call manic or psychotic behavior was caused by demons, malicious spirits who took up residence within human beings. We must also note that the evil spirits immediately recognized the divine power in Jesus' spirit (8:29), compared to the often slow-witted disciples. It was further believed that when the messiah came, he would destroy the demons. Until then they had free rein. Hence the question, *Have you come here to torment us before the time?* (NRSV; NIV = *torture us before the appointed time?*) Jesus demonstrated his authority and power to command these demons to leave the two men. We have seen Jesus' power over disease, over the elements of the storm, and now we see his control over demonic spirits.

The destruction of the herd of swine (pigs, which are

considered to be unclean animals) may have been a separate story that became attached to this incident with the demons. There may have been the belief that in no other way could the demons be destroyed except by driving them into the animals who then drowned in the sea. People could identify the unclean animals and the water as an appropriate setting for such destruction. Above all the details, the truth emerges clearly: Jesus has power over evil spirits.

Healing a Paralytic (9:1-8)

This last of the second luster of these mighty works (the storm, the demoniacs, the paralytic) introduces some themes of central importance to Matthew. Two dimensions are constant in all the healing stories: the faith of those who bring the afflicted person, and Jesus' compassion. His response to their trust is no less important than his pity. But this is the first instance in this Gospel of Jesus forgiving sins. Here begins the unceasing conflict between Jesus and the religious authorities. It was on the issue of blasphemy that Jesus stood charged in his final trial (26:65).

Matthew's version of the incident is shorter than Mark's (Mark 2:1-12). What Matthew chiefly emphasizes is Jesus' claim that he had the authority to forgive sin (9:6). The Jews understood that in the day-to-day exchanges of life persons could and should forgive each other. But what aroused the ire and fear of the scribes in this situation was Jesus' assertion that directly from God, he, a mortal human being, had received power to forgive a man the sins that had caused his paralysis. No one questioned in those days that all sickness, including paralysis, was due to sin. Until the sins had been forgiven, wholeness could not be restored. We might call it psychosomatic healing of a functional paralysis. Whatever it may be called, the removal of sin and guilt was crucial. Only God could do that. So when Jesus did it, the scribes were appalled. Jesus was acting as God's representative among men and women. This was blasphemy.

If we have here the verbatim words of Jesus, and we have no reason to think otherwise, the authorities were offended by the messianic title *Son of man.* By contrast the crowds *glorified God* (NRSV; NIV = *praised God).* Of course, the rulers of the synagogue were afraid such a person would threaten their own authority and following.

Ceremonial Purity and Fasting (9:9-17)

The calling of Matthew is of more than incidental interest. Jesus gave witness by this act that the gospel was for all people, not just the ceremonially righteous. Tax collectors were among the people most despised by the religious authorities. Mark and Luke identify the tax collector called to be a disciple as Levi. Scholars have disagreed as to whether these were two names for the same person. We have no way of knowing how much, if anything, the tax collector Matthew had to do with compiling or writing the Gospel.

The call of such an "outsider" is well-placed to introduce the controversy that follows, perhaps in Matthew's own house. For devout Jews to "sit at table" with tax collectors and non-observant Jews (sinners) offended the guardians of Jewish purity. Knowing the offense of his behavior to the Pharisees, Jesus quotes from Hosea 6:6: *I desire steadfast love [mercy] and not sacrifice. Steadfast love* (mercy), in Jesus' mind, involving healing and forgiveness. That Jesus actually went out seeking sinners compounded the offense.

The iniquity by disciples of John the Baptist points directly at the dividing line between John and Jesus. When Jesus used the word *bridegroom,* he employed a messianic symbol. A wedding feast was frequently used as a metaphor for the messianic banquet in the age to come. What can Jesus mean here but that he, the bridegroom (Messiah) is still with them? Guests always rejoice as long as the groom remains with them. In those days wedding feasts frequently lasted for several days. *The days* (NRSV; NIV = *time*) *will come when the bridegroom is taken away*—Jesus' first veiled reference to his death. The inference is clear: Now that Jesus has come, there is no further need for John to gather his own disciples.

Nor can new cloth be stitched onto the old, or new wine be put in old wineskins to ferment. The old covenant cannot contain the new wine of the gospel. Both old and new can only be preserved if they are separated.

Four Healings (9:18-34)

The *ruler* (NIV; NRSV = *leader*) was very likely an official of some kind in the community. Both Mark's account (Mark 5:21-43) and Matthew's indicate that the girl had died before Jesus came to the ruler's house. If this is true, it is the first instance where Jesus raises someone from the dead. Nothing better demonstrates the authority of Jesus than his power over death and life, the point of a person's ultimate need. We cannot be sure how to read Jesus' saying that *the girl is not dead but asleep* (NIV, verse 24), found also in both Luke and Mark. *Sleep* is a metaphor for death found in both the Old and New Testaments. It is not clear whether Jesus recognizes the girl to be in a coma, or whether he is saying that death no longer holds anyone with finality. The people believed that Jesus had recalled the girl from real death. It is hard to read that Matthew had any other intention.

The healing of a woman with a hemorrhage (verses 20-22) occurred both as a result of faith—*if I only touch his cloak*—and from the touch itself. Luke tells us that Jesus felt power go out of him.

The story of the two blind men parallels the account of the healing of blind Bartimaeus at Jericho (Matthew 20:29-34; Mark 10:46-52). As with all the healings in Matthew, the stress is on faith. Jesus demands that they confess their faith; healing is not automatic. Notice that they address Jesus as *Son of David* and as *Lord*—two messianic titles.

The demoniac (verses 32-34) was *mute* (NRSV) in the sense that he could not talk (NIV). The people marveled when they heard him speak. The Pharisees charged that Jesus was in league with the devil, the prince of demons. This charge is made the central issue in the controversy reported in Matthew 12:22-32.

Summary (9:35-38)

In chapters 5–7 Matthew has set forth the *teachings* of Jesus of which the disciples were to be the bearers. In chapters 8–9 Jesus has demonstrated the *healing* ministry with which they were also to be charged. Jesus acknowledges here that he alone cannot carry out the mission for which he has been sent into the world. Like the owner of a vineyard, Jesus needs help to gather the harvest. He also draws on a familiar Old Testament figure—the sheep and the shepherd (Numbers 27:17; Psalm 28:9; Isaiah 40:11; Jeremiah 23:1-8).

§ § § § § § §

The Message of Matthew 8–9

Matthew arranged his Gospel to include ten so-called miracles at this point. He did that for one reason: *to support the faith that Jesus did speak and act with the authority of God.* The miracles are not reported to prove that Jesus was a wonder worker, an exorcist, or one with power to control the weather. The mighty works were not in themselves the main purpose or wonder of the incidents. There were many exorcists and magicians of all kinds in the ancient world. But Jesus did these wonderful things always *in response to the faith of the afflicted persons or those who brought them to Jesus.* Whether we believe the miracle stories as literal accounts of what happened, or as symbolic stories to convey a truth about the spirit and power of one who came in the name of God, they can be for us what they were for the first Christians. They can be images of what God still does for those who come with confidence and trust.

God's power is spiritual. Faith transfigures that power into physical and material effects. This does not mean that *we* do it all by the act of faith. Sometimes God acts even before persons have faith, as in the calming of the storm, and the healing of the two demoniacs. In these two instances faith followed the mighty works. Nor does it mean that everything will happen just as we want it, even with great faith. It does mean that through faith God can cleanse us, reduce the fevers of life, quiet our fears in the face of life's storms, rebuke the demons that plague us, forgive us so we are no longer paralyzed by our guilt and sins, restore our sight, and lead us out of death into new life.

When the Gadarenes saw the herd of swine plunge into the sea (8:32), they were upset, as well we might expect them to be. To lose a whole herd of animals was to lose one's livelihood. This is not the main point of the story, nor is it even a detail by which we evaluate Jesus. The story raises more troublesome questions. From the day forward Jesus has always disturbed the communities into which he has come. He comes with comfort, as he did for the two demoniacs. But he comes also to change our values, our expectations, and our commitments. When these change, there is no telling how upset we will be, sometimes even begging him to leave our neighborhood (8:34).

§ § § § § § § §

Matthew 10

Introduction to This Chapter

Chapter 10 contains the teaching discourse of Matthew's second section. The teaching is more sharply focused here than in the more general discourses (chapters 5–7, 13, 18, 24–25): Jesus speaks to the disciples about the mission on which he is about to send them.

Three strands of purpose bind this chapter into a unity: *requirements*—how they are to carry on the mission (5-15); *responses*—what they will encounter in the way of welcome and rejection (16-25); and *rewards*—what consequences they may expect from the mission (26-42).

But beyond this briefing of the disciples about their mission, Jesus addresses the church in the time after the first mission has ended. His words to his disciples are also words to his followers "on mission" in the Apostolic Age after the first disciples have passed on. Also in this chapter is Matthew's list of the twelve disciples.

The rewards Jesus promises are without comparison, but the dangers, difficulties, and distress that his disciples must face are sufficient to discourage all but the most stout-hearted.

Here is an outline of chapter 10.
  I. Commissioning the Apostles (10:1-4)
 II. Requirements (10:5-15)
III. Responses to Be Expected (10:16-25)
IV. Rewards and Consequences (10:26-42)

Commissioning the Apostles (10:1-4)

Jesus confers upon the disciples the authority that he has demonstrated in his own mighty works, to cast out unclean spirits and heal every disease.

Matthew's list of the disciples is identical with Mark's, while Luke omits Thaddaeus in favor of Judas (not Iscariot), son of James. Most of these disciples are not mentioned again in the New Testament. Matthew did not have as much interest in them as individuals as he had in the group of twelve as a whole. The number twelve matches the number of tribes of Israel. Mark 6:7 gives us the detail, omitted by Matthew, that Jesus sent them out two by two. But the listing of the names in pairs implies that two disciples journeyed together.

An *apostle* is "one who is sent on a mission." Matthew does not use the word elsewhere in his Gospel, but it occurs frequently in Luke and Acts, and often in the letters of Paul. *Disciple* means literally "one who follows and learns." The two words can usually be interchanged. One cannot be an apostle without having been a disciple, and none can be disciples who are not also missionaries. The title *apostle* was rarely used in Scripture except to refer to the original twelve.

Requirements (10:5-15)

We have already seen that non-Jews can and do respond to the good news. At the end of the Gospel (28:19) and in Acts 1:8 the field is declared to be the whole world. The question might then be raised of why this restriction of the field to Israel here? It is not really a contradiction. In 10:6 and again in 15:24 Jesus announces that he has been sent to the lost sheep of Israel. Apparently the earliest followers, and Jesus himself, believed that the gospel must first be preached to Israel. Then, after its rejection by the Jews, apostles could go to the Gentiles. Jesus himself, as though anticipating what would happen in the days following his death, often mingled with non-Jews and commended their faith. But the ministry of apostles (the outreach of the church) was to be to Israel in Jesus' lifetime.

Were the *lost sheep* the Jews who failed to observe the laws? Hardly the case, considering Jesus' controversy with the scribes and Pharisees. Or did Jesus mean all who would not respond to his gospel? In either case the gospel was first preached to Jews.

The directives in verses 7-10 tell us several things about the apostolic assignment. Obviously it was not for the faint-hearted. Nor were they to anticipate a settled ministry anywhere. People centuries later who followed this model were called "circuit riders," not remaining long in one place. The fact that there was much work to do but few workers (9:37) made it essential for those few to keep moving on. They were to take no baggage, no money, few possessions. As they went, they were to do all the things Jesus had been doing (10:7-8). The text makes clear that the disciples were to be fed and their needs attended to by the people among whom they ministered (10:11). The whole passage indicates the expectation of the early appearance of the Son of man (10:23).

One saluted a house with the greeting, "Peace be to this house." If the greeting was not received, the disciple was to move on to another house (verse 13).

Deserving (worthy) does not signify a moral judgment, but rather one who was willing to entertain an apostle (but see the discussion under 10:37-38).

When Jews returned from Gentile territory, they performed the ritual of shaking off the dust so as not to defile the land of Israel. Houses where the apostles were not received they considered heathen and unclean, whose dust must be shaken off (verse 14). Since the apostles came with the authority of Jesus, when any town or house rejected them, it rejected the Lord (see 10:40).

Sodom and Gomorrah had become symbols for places consigned to obliteration (Genesis 18:16–19:28).

Responses to Be Expected (10:16-25)

Jesus addresses these words to the disciples. When Matthew reports the warnings, it is with the apostolic church in mind, and all the churches that would follow it. Let them be aware! Whenever Christ's disciples go into the world preaching, teaching, and healing, they will be *like sheep among wolves* (verse 16), defenseless as sheep among predatory beasts, without the physical presence of a shepherd; *taken before officials* (verse 18), the local authorities charged with enforcing adherence to Jewish law; and hated because they are his followers. (verse 22).

Testimony before Gentiles, of course, foresees Jesus on trial before Pilate, and Christians everywhere who refuse to bend the knee or lift the hand in salute to pagan culture.

Christians go into the world in the name of Jesus. To bear the name of Jesus is to be with God's Spirit and God's power. So the apostles may expect that Spirit to speak through them when they are brought to testify.

If verse 23 *(before the Son of man comes)* is an authentic word of Jesus, to what did he refer? The Passion and Resurrection that awaited him? The end time when the Messiah would finally appear in all his glory? When Matthew incorporated the prediction at this point in the Gospel written for the Church, he knew Jesus' exaltation in the Resurrection. He looked forward to the end-time, and he shared the urgency of wanting to see all of Israel evangelized before the event. It is difficult to accept the idea that Jesus believed in the literal coming of the end-time while the apostles were still on their first mission, and before his own death!

Matthew and the churches for whom this gospel was prepared knew what lay ahead for Jesus. Christians of that later day understood what it meant for a servant to be like the master (10:24). The reference to Beelzebul recalls what the Pharisees had said: *It is by the prince of demons that he casts out demons.* (NIV 9:34).

Rewards and Consequences (10:26-42)

To consider the promises of Jesus to the disciples as *compensation* would be too weak a word, as though it were a payoff for those who endure. *Fulfillment* is a stronger word. The faithful disciples fulfill God's purpose for their lives. They become *perfect* (5:48); this is reward surpassing any other. Any "disciple" who denies the Lord will find nothing offered by God in heaven that he or she ever cares to inherit or stand for.

The sayings in verses 34-36 are difficult. Christian disciples must know that faithfulness to Jesus Christ will divide families. Deepest loyalties and family ties will be shaken and superceded by ties of the Kingdom. The sword that Jesus brings is not the sword of conquest, but the sword of division, a sword that demands a choice: Whom will you serve? (See "The Message of Matthew 10.")

One who is *not worthy* of Jesus (verses 37-38) is one who is unfit for discipleship. Being unworthy has more to do with being qualified for discipleship than with moral rectitude. If personal ties will restrain a man or woman from ultimate commitment to Jesus, that person is not fit to be a disciple.

In verse 38 Jesus speaks of the cross for the first time in Matthew's Gospel. This verse has been called "prophecy after the event." Matthew's church knew what it meant to "take up the cross." Even so, Jesus surely understood that he and his disciples each faced the probability of violent death, perhaps execution by Roman authorities.

Whoever loses his life for my sake (NIV, verse 39) is found in all four Gospels, twice in both Matthew and Luke, once in Mark and John. We read it as further exposition of 5:10-11—the disciple risks life for Jesus' sake and inherits the Kingdom.

Jesus further underlines the unique status of the disciples/apostles. They go with the authority of Jesus, whose authority comes directly from God. He is saying that people who receive the disciples give hospitality to God's presence and Spirit.

A prophet's reward has frequently been death. The righteous may be persecuted for righteousness' sake. To give a cup of cold water to *the least* of Christ's brothers is to minister to him (25:40). Another translation might be: Whoever gives to one of the most insignificant of these a mere cup of water does the same for Christ. Jesus leaves no doubt that whether one receives a prophet or gives a cup of water to a humble disciple, the reward is the same.

§ § § § § § §

The Message of Matthew 10

Being a disciple is a job having few equals: tough
things to do; opposition everywhere you go; flogged even
in the holy places, if not physically, yet psychologically
and emotionally; being hated for Christ's sake;
separation from your own family; and may be a cross as
your reward at the end. So what is there to love about it?

The certainty that the Christ will acknowledge me (call
me his disciple) before God; confidence that the life I
may lose for Jesus' sake I can never balance against the
life I will find with him. Those rewards are still in effect
for anyone who becomes a Christian disciple.

I have not come to bring peace but a sword (NRSV, 10:34).
This text has been misused across the centuries. People
have quoted it in a military context, as though Jesus
thereby sanctioned war. But Jesus was not referring to
military or political matters. We cannot make ethical
decisions about violence by quoting this verse. Jesus
knew that loyalty to him would divide families as though
a great sword had cleaved the fabric of relationships.
Fidelity to Jesus must supercede every other commitment.

A Christian disciple will learn the art of both receiving
and giving. These two acts are like the systolic and
diastolic beats of the human heart. We are to receive one
who comes in the name (that is, in the Spirit, the
purpose) of the Lord. We are to receive the prophet (one
who speaks for God.) We are to receive the righteous
person (the good person with loving intentions). We are
also to give, even the humble offering of a cup of water,
to someone in need. We receive in order that we may
give; we give that others may receive. The cycle of
receiving and giving has no closing and no ending.

§ § § § § § §

Matthew 11–12

Introduction to These Chapters

The Gospel returns in chapters 11–12 to the narrative of Jesus' ministry as he moves into a new stage of opposition and rejection by the synagogue leaders. Matthew tells us nothing about the results of the apostles' mission, if indeed they have yet gone. It may be that the briefing in chapter 10 looked forward to the Great Commission in Matthew 28:16-20. The "hidden revelation" serves as a general title of the whole of the third section of the Gospel (chapters 11–13).

According to Matthew, Jesus reveals by several disclosures that he is the one who has been anticipated. (11:4-6, 27; 12:6, 8, 28, 41-42). In these two chapters we observe the widening rift between the religious authorities and his new followers (verse 25). All this leads up to chapter 13, where the hidden meaning of the Kingdom is revealed through parables.

In chapter 11 Jesus speaks to the crowds about John the Baptist, who has inquired from prison, *Are you the one who is to come?* (NRSV, verse 3). Jesus condemns the cities where people have not responded to his revelation, and he invites the crowds to come to him to *find rest for your souls* (11:29).

Chapter 12 takes us into three controversies with the Pharisees, each of which prompts a repeated indication of who Jesus is (12:8, 18, 23). The concluding verse sums

it up: *For whoever does the will of my Father in heaven is my brother, and sister, and mother.*
Here is an outline of chapters 11–12.
  I. Jesus and John the Baptist (11:2-19)
 II. Woe to Unrepentant Cities (11:2-19)
III. Self-revelation of Jesus (11:25-30)
 IV. Opposition by the Pharisees (12:1-45)
  V. Jesus' True Family (12:46-50)

Jesus and John the Baptist (11:2-19)

From John's question sent by his disciples to Jesus *(Are you the one who is to come?)*, we infer that John was not sure whether Jesus was the messiah for whom Israel waited. Jesus certainly had not fulfilled these hopes. It would be surprising if John did not wonder. In reply to the question Jesus points to the mighty works reported in chapters 8–9. He leaves it to John to draw his own conclusions that these things happened in fulfillment of Isaiah 35:5-6 and 61:1. *Takes no offense* (NRSV, verse 6) could be translated *is repelled by nothing in me*, or, as found in the NIV, *does not fall away on account of me.* Jesus may not expect John to become a disciple of such an unfamiliar kind of messiah; he will be content if John does not find Jesus to be a stumbling block.

Jesus now turns to the crowds in praise of John. That they understand clearly who John was is pivotal to their awareness of who Jesus is. In a sense Jesus drives the people back into their own experience of John in the wilderness (chapter 3) in order for them to recapture the realization of John as the forerunner of Jesus. Jesus asks them, Did you go out to see a man wavering like a reed in the wind? Or a man living in fine clothes? Or did you go out to see a prophet? Of course, a prophet! In fact, the prophet of whom Malachi spoke, *who would prepare the way before me* (Malachi 3:1). Matthew changes the Malachi verse from *before me to before you.*

Jesus' question to the crowds may be a reinforcement

for John if his faith is now blowing in the wind. In the wilderness John did not waver in the wind nor take his ease lying in fine clothes. John needs to remember this; so do the people. Because John immediately preceded Jesus, preparing the way for him, John ranks higher than all those who came before him. He was the last in the succession of witnesses in the old covenant. With Jesus a new covenant begins. The least of those who enter this Kingdom is greater than any forerunner could ever be. Jesus makes this distinction not to put John down, but to stress the radical new age that Jesus was inaugurating. Jesus recognizes in John the promised return of Elijah (11:14; Malachi 4:5).

If verse 12 is a true word of Jesus, how shall we understand it? There had been little violence between the time of John's appearing and the present in which Jesus speaks. For this reason, and the fact that nothing else in Jesus' teachings is anything like this, many scholars have concluded that we have here not Jesus' words, but words of Matthew. Matthew's Gospel may have appeared as much as fifty years after John the Baptist. There had certainly been a great deal of violence in that period, beginning with the Crucifixion itself.

Moreover, it is impossible to know whether the words mean that men have continually tried to seize the Kingdom by violent means, or whether it says that the Kingdom can only be entered by those who will seize it with great spiritual force. One way or the other, violent power attends the appearance of the kingdom of heaven. Jesus knew that!

Both John and Jesus are criticized and rejected. John was criticized by people because he fasted. Jesus was rejected by the authorities because he feasted. John was said to have a demon. Jesus was accused of being in league with Beelzebul because he sought out tax collectors and non-observing Jews.

Wisdom (verse 19) probably means the wisdom of God

is justified by results. This seems to be another way of saying, "By their fruits you shall know them." A popular maxim has it that "the proof of the pudding is in the eating." Look at both John and Jesus and see what they did. God's wisdom is justified by them both.

Woe to Unrepentant Cities (11:20-24)

Chorazin (Korazin) was a city north of Capernaum; it is not mentioned elsewhere in the New Testament. Bethsaida was east of Capernaum on the shore of Galilee. It is mentioned on a number of occasions as a scene in Jesus' ministry. On all three towns Jesus delivered scathing judgment, the like of which fell upon Tyre and Sidon, two Gentile cities, and Sodom, a place of notorious wickedness (Genesis 19:24-25). These verses send a warning to Israel to respond to the mighty works of Jesus with repentance and faith.

Self-revelation of Jesus (11:25-30)

In verses 25-26 Jesus rejoices and gives thanks that God has revealed so much of the way, the truth, and the life to *little children (infants)*, and that they have received it in faith. The *wise* and *learned (intelligent)* are the scribes and religious authorities who do not receive it.

The next two verses (27-28) sound more like the Gospel of John than Matthew (see John 1:1-18). They are unique in all the synoptic Gospels in voicing Jesus' claim that *no one knows the Father except the Son* (verse 27). These lines may be an outburst of faith from a first-century Christian that found their way into the earliest tradition.

The invitation (verses 28-30) could be the call of Jesus to all the heavy-laden who labor under the Jewish law, and under Phariseeism as a whole. The metaphor of the *yoke* is a vivid way of saying, "My way fits you well." (The burden of faith will be light compared to the legalism of the Pharisees: See "The Message of Matthew 11–12.")

Opposition by the Pharisees (12:1-45)

The incident of plucking grain on the sabbath (verses 1-8) may appear to us as much ado about nothing. Why would a minor infraction of one of the thirty-nine laws covering work on the sabbath stir up such a controversy? But plucking a few ears of corn was only the pretext for the Pharisees to condemn Jesus for the authority that he claimed to exercise. They perceived in Jesus' violation of sabbath rules an unacceptable transgression of the laws by which Israel maintained the covenant. Jesus challenged them with three precedents and a claim for his own authority.

First, David ate the bread of the Presence. This bread was placed in the sanctuary at the beginning of the sabbath, where it remained until the following sabbath, when the priests were permitted to eat it (see 1 Samuel 21:1-6). Furthermore, asks Jesus, if the priests profane the sabbath with impunity, how can it be wrong for me and my disciples? Jesus is greater even than the Temple. This staggering claim the Pharisees could not tolerate.

As he had done when they condemned him for eating with non-observing Jews, Jesus again quotes Hoses 6:6: *I desire mercy and not sacrifice.*

The Son of Man is lord of the sabbath (12:8) was the ultimate blasphemy. There is a general consensus among scholars that Mark's Gospel has the original ending to this confrontation: *The sabbath was made for humankind, not humankind for the sabbath* (NRSV, Mark 2:27). The messianic claim made by Jesus would have become part of the tradition to which the early church appealed in its controversy with the Jewish authorities of that later period.

The same conflict lies at the heart of the next incident, in which Jesus heals a person on the sabbath (verses 9-14). Jesus invokes the imperative of mercy above sacrifice. Since Jewish law permitted kindness to animals on the sabbath, how much more should we be encouraged to show mercy to human beings! There is a technicality here. In matters of emergency, life and death, one could intervene on the sabbath. The man with the withered hand could have waited until sundown. The demonstration Jesus gave by healing the man overrode the prescription. Mercy could not give way to technicalities!

That Matthew should here introduce a passage from one of the servant songs of Isaiah of the Exile (Isaiah 42:1-4) reveals a turning point in the Christian mission in his own day. We know from Paul's letters and from Acts that the mission to the Gentiles had begun to bear fruit. As Jesus was repeatedly, and with ever greater severity, rejected by the leaders of Israel, the prophecy from Isaiah appropriately validates turning to the Gentiles. Matthew pictures Jesus turning to those who needed justice and hope (12:20-21).

Following Jesus' healing of the blind and dumb man, the Pharisees launched an even more venomous attack. *It is only by Beelzebul, the prince of demons, that this fellow drives out demons* (NIV, verse 24). Jesus demolishes their charge by the illogic of a kingdom divided against itself, and by the question, What about your sons? We reach the summit of this chapter in the affirmation that *the kingdom of God has come upon you* (NIV, verse 28). Jesus already ties up *the strong man* (that is, the devil).

For discussion of 12:31-32 see "The Message of Matthew 11–12."

The roots of the saying, *The good news brings forth good fruit* (verses 33-37) tap deep into the soil of the Sermon on the Mount (Matthew 7:16-20). A person's words and behavior come out of inner attitudes. Character is revealed in words and deeds that express the inner commitments and loyalties of the soul.

For the second and third time in this chapter we hear the words, *One greater than (the Temple, Jonah, Solomon) is here* (NIV, 12:6, 41, 42). Here again the Gospel proclaims that in Jesus, God has come into the human scene in a new and greater way than ever before. Matthew sends these words to his church at the time of their harassment by the authorities as a way of saying: In Jesus the Christ God offers a new covenant, fulfilling the hope of long ages; listen to the preaching, greater than Jonah's, and attend to the wisdom, wiser than Solomon's.

It was believed that a demon, once cast out of a person, sought to return. If the mind and soul thereafter remained empty the demon would not only find the old lodging, but would bring other demons with him. And the last state of that person would be worse than the first. We can see here how much Jesus understood of psychosomatic medicine and the problems of addiction, although these things were called then by other names.

Jesus' True Family (12:46-50)

How easy to associate this episode with the statement in John 7:5: *Even his brothers did not believe in him.* Neither Matthew nor Mark make any such implication here, although it may well have been true. Nor do they suggest that Jesus' own family thought he was *out of his mind*, as some of Jesus' friends apparently believed (Mark 3:21). Jesus does not repudiate his family in this encounter. Rather, he uses the occasion to include in his family people everywhere who receive him.

§ § § § § § §

The Message of Matthew 11–12

The beatitude in Matthew 11:6 comes across the centuries independently of the Sermon on the Mount. A blessing awaits the persons who find no offense in Jesus and who are not put off by what different people do in the name of Jesus: giving the blind their sight, giving the lame the power to walk, healing disease, offering new life to the dying (in spirit as well as body), the gift of hearing to the deaf, preaching justice and mercy to the poor. We are blessed if we take no offense at anything the Spirit of Christ continues to do in the world.

Jesus says, *If any want to become my followers, let them deny themselves and take up their cross and follow me.* (NRSV, 16:24). He also says, *My yoke is easy, and my burden is light* (11:30). This is a paradox: two opposites that, by logic, cannot both be true. But both statements are true in a way that transcends logic. What Jesus says is this: If you trust my promises, the gospel will fit you. You will be able to carry heavy burdens, even the burden of the cross, with comfort (strength).

Ever since Jesus said that whoever speaks against the Holy Spirit will not be forgiven, people have worried, wondering, Have I committed the sin that God will not forgive? The answer almost invariably is, no, not in the sense of there being a particular act or sin that God will not forgive. But it is possible for a person to so close his or her heart to the promptings of God's Holy Spirit that he or she no longer knows the truth. When we reach the point where we call evil good and good evil, then forgiveness will have neither meaning nor healing. It is not that God will not give, rather it is that we cannot receive.

§ § § § § § §

Matthew 13

Introduction to This Chapter

Chapter 13 forms the teaching discourse of Matthew's third section. It is the only one of the five teaching sections of the Gospel explicitly directed to the crowds. Seven parables are here, together with interpretations of two of them, and two explanations of why Jesus taught in parables.

Notwithstanding that the parables have their dark side—the seeds that do not germinate, the fire that will consume the weeds, and the bad fish that will be thrown out—the principal emphasis in this chapter is on the Kingdom. When people hear the word and understand it, the gospel brings forth a rich harvest. The Lord will come at the final harvest and gather the faithful into the Kingdom. And that gathering is worth every price one can pay, every exchange that could possibly be made.

A parable is a brief story (such as 13:24-30), a metaphor (13:31-33), or simile (13:44-50) that conveys a truth about life. The parable is an illustration taken from one familiar realm of life whose truth can be applied to another realm. The wheat and the weeds are not really about agriculture, but through that story the listener can see the truth about good and bad growing together before the time of judgment. The leaven is not really about baking, but about the word of God that transforms all of life. The story of the pearl of great value is not about pearl diving but about the supreme value of the kingdom of heaven.

Jesus used parables in much of his teaching, especially teaching about the kingdom of God.

Here is an outline of chapter 13.

I. The Sower (13:3-9, 18-23)
II. Why Jesus Taught in Parables (13:10-17, 34-35)
III. The Wheat and the Weeds (13:24-30, 36-43)
IV. The Mustard Seed and the Leaven (13:31-33)
V. The Pearl and the Net (13:44-50)
VI. Scribes Trained for the Kingdom (13:51-52)
VII. Jesus Teaches in His Own Country (13:53-58)

The Sower (13:3-9, 18-23)

This parable is not so much about the sower as it is about the soils; the comparison to which the story points is among the several kinds of soil into which the seed falls. The soils represent the different ways Jesus' teaching falls into human "soils."

Seeds, perhaps blown by the wind to an open path, are readily spotted by the birds and devoured. Farmers today find it strange that the seed was scattered before the soil was plowed and prepared. Soil yielding a hundredfold was considered astonishingly fruitful.

In verses 18-23 Jesus explains the parable of the sower. This parable and the next one (the wheat and the weeds) are the only two of his parables that Jesus explained. Why just these two? Partly because of the difference between parable and allegory. A parable is a story or metaphor that makes a single point. The details of the story are of no significance except as they contribute to the single meaning. In an allegory all the details have symbolic meaning. Jesus didn't tell allegories, except as later tradition turned his parables into allegories. Jesus told parables. They needed no explanation. Indeed, it is the nature of parables to so involve the listeners in the story that they discern the meaning for themselves. One of the best examples of this kind of teaching, really confrontation, is the parable of the poor man and his ewe lamb that the prophet Nathan told to David in the Old Testament to compel David to convict himself of his sin against Uriah and Bathsheba (2 Samuel 12:1-7).

Jesus may have explained this parable to the disciples privately, as he did with the wheat and the weeds, in order to help explain the contrasting responses with which his teachings were met. Much of what he taught, which the apostles were in turn to teach, was choked by thorns or scorched for lack of soil. It would be disheartening to preach with such discouraging results. So Jesus reminded the disciples of the hundredfold harvest that God would gather at the end time of judgment.

Why Jesus Taught in Parables (13:10-17, 34-35)

These verses are confusing, to say the least. First of all, Isaiah's prophecy was pointed at the people whose hearts had grown dull, whose ears had become heavy, and whose eyes were closed, so that they failed to understand God's word (Isaiah 6:9-10). The same could have been said of Israel in its response to Jesus. In fact, Matthew is saying just that. But verse 14, echoing Mark 4:12, seems to imply that Jesus told the parables with the deliberate intention that people would *not* understand. This does not square with anything else in the Gospels about how Jesus taught and the way he reached out to the "lost sheep" who were without a shepherd.

We can read verse 13 something like this: I speak to them in parables so that they can see what you see, but which is now hidden from them, and so that they can understand what they have heard. Jesus quotes Psalm 78:1-4 as a precedent for doing exactly that. The whole Christian mission, beginning with the sending out of the apostles, contradicts any idea that the gospel consisted of a kind of esoteric knowledge that could be known only by a select few who were given the key to understanding. The parables did not need explanations to make their meaning clear.

The Wheat and the Weeds (13:24-30, 36-43)

This parable probes the mystery of how evil gets mixed in with good, especially in the church. Matthew uses Jesus' words to address the problem that plagued the apostolic church: How should they deal with evil and good side by side?

The weeds were probably darnel, a noxious weed, which in its early growth so closely resembled wheat that it was hard to distinguish the two. The parable points to the dilemma of evil and good being much alike in many ways in their early stages. The parable says that an enemy sowed the seeds *while everyone was sleeping.* When the parable is turned into an allegory, the enemy (the devil) becomes a significant symbol. But even without an enemy, weeds mysteriously sprout everywhere. We live in that kind of world. The main thrust of the parable is toward the harvest, the time of final judgment when the wheat will be separated from the weeds. Here, as in earlier passages, Jesus condemns the evildoers to *the furnace where there will be weeping and gnashing of teeth* (verse 42). This parable does not try to persuade people not to cultivate their gardens. It hopes to encourage the apostolic church in its bewilderment over evil mixed in with good in its congregations.

The Mustard Seed and the Leaven (13:31-33)

These two parables about the future are often misinterpreted to mean that the Kingdom grows gradually, like seeds into trees, or leaven causing bread to rise. Nothing could be further from Matthew's conviction or from the mind of Jesus. The idea of a slowly evolving kingdom of heaven on earth was utterly alien to first-century followers of Jesus Christ. Everywhere the expectation anticipated the sudden appearance of the messiah and the time of final judgment. The contrast was between the tiny, almost inconspicuous beginnings in the teaching of Israel and preaching to the Gentiles, on the one hand, and on the other the mighty tree that would appear at the harvest. Likewise the invisible leaven hidden in the meal causes the whole loaf to rise. The Spirit of God is already at work, sometimes hidden in the world. Normally, leaven was used as a metaphor for evil influence. Leaven corrupted people, causing evil desires. Jesus turns the parable inside out, using the word as metaphor for yeast. These are parables to encourage the faith of the disciples. Despite appearances, the power of God will fulfill all righteousness. And that unseen power the disciples can trust without misgiving, as they trust the energy in the tiny seed and the mysterious leavening power in the yeast.

The Pearl and the Net (13:44-50)

The similes *(The kingdom of heaven is like . . .)* point to the disciplines to which the disciples must submit and the supreme value of the Kingdom above all other possessions.

We take note of the fact that in the first parable the man finds the treasure quite by accident. The merchant, on the other hand, has searched all his life for the precious pearl; finally he comes upon it. We may take these stories to mean that persons find the Kingdom and enter it in different ways. Both men have this in common, however: They recognize the supreme value of the Kingdom when they discover it. It transcends every other value; no price is too great to pay, not even selling everything (verses 44-46).

The net is similar to the wheat and the weeds. The harvest from the sea is like the harvest from the field; all kinds of fish come up in the net. Jesus is saying to the disciples here: You cannot separate the good from the bad while you preach. That differentiation must be left to God. We cannot see down the road. When the day of reckoning finally comes, God will decide. There will be an abundant catch in the net. Our work will not have been in vain.

Jesus Teaches in His Own Country (13:53-58)

This section describes the rejection Jesus encounters as he preaches in his own territory. The two final verses point vividly to a surprising truth. Often it happens that Jesus can perform no mighty works around us precisely because we have taken offense at things Jesus has done. Or we have given offense by just ignoring him!

§ § § § § § §

The Message of Matthew 13

When the Word falls into good soil it brings forth an abundant harvest. The gospel assures me that this will happen in my own life when I receive the Word. It will happen also in whole communities of people. The Word has power when it is given lodging and nurture.

Christians have always had to live with the tension between patience and zeal. We are tempted when we see evil to rush in and pull it up by the roots. At times that may be necessary. But sometimes the wisdom of Jesus dictates that we be patient. Tearing up evil can sometimes destroy fragile goodness trying to take root and grow, especially in a community like the church.

Who would suppose, looking at a tiny mustard seed, that all the potential for a great shrub lies within that seed? So it is with the Word of God. Seemingly fleeting and fragile, yet what transformations it has wrought in the life of the world!

The Lord's power to heal may depend on our will to receive. To the faith of the one who receives is bound the power of the one who gives. When Jesus does not do for us what he has done elsewhere, maybe the reason lies in the offense we take at and give to him.

§ § § § § § §

Matthew 14–15

Introduction to These Chapters

Section four of Matthew's Gospel is the charter for
the Christian church. In the narrative section
(14:1–17:27) Jesus rejects the rule of the Pharisees and
Sadducees (15:12-14; 16:1-12), embraces the Gentiles in
his ministry (15:21-29), acknowledges that he is the
Christ (16:17), ordains Peter as the rock on which he
will build his church, and announces his death and
resurrection. Chapter 18 is a manual of discipline for
church members.

Chapters 14–15 include reports of events leading up to
the climactic revelations and announcements of chapter
16. We read first how Herod Antipas murdered John the
Baptist. Next comes the account of Jesus feeding more
than five thousand people in a lonely place. During
another storm on the Sea of Galilee Jesus comes to the
disciples across the water. Again Jesus finds himself in
controversies with the Pharisees over ritual cleanliness.
Finally, we read a report of feeding four thousand in the
region of the Gentiles.

Here is an outline of chapters 14–15.
   I. Murder of John the Baptist (14:1-12)
  II. Jesus' Miraculous Works (14:13-36)
      A. Feeding the five thousand (14:13-21)
      B. Jesus walks on the water (14:22-27)
      C. Peter's little faith (14:28-33)
      D. Jesus heals many (14:34-36)

III. Controversy Over Ritual Cleanliness (15:1-20)

IV. Encounter with Gentiles (15:21-39)

Murder of John the Baptist (14:1-12)

Our first encounter with the Herods was with Herod the Great (king of Judea 37-4 B.C.), who slaughtered the innocents in Bethlehem at the time of Jesus' birth (2:13-18). Now we meet one of Herod's sons, Herod Antipas, who carried on the Herodian violence with his brutal murder of John the Baptist. Antipas was tetrarch of Galilee and the Transjordan, the land lying east of the Jordan River. He ruled that region under the aegis of Rome. The Herods were Jews by lineal descent, but they collaborated with Rome in suppressing the Jewish nation. The Jews held them in contempt.

Josephus, first-century Jewish historian whose writing was contemporary with the formation of the Christian Scriptures, says that Herod feared John the Baptist's influence over the people. Afraid that it might lead to revolt, he decided to execute John before things got beyond his control.

Mark (Mark 6:14-19) and Matthew add the additional reason for John's murder: John denounced Herod for his marriage to Herodias, his half-brother Philip's wife. Leviticus 20:21 forbids a man to take his brother's wife. According to the Gospel story, Herodias was so incensed by John's condemnation that she plotted to do away with John. The occasion came at a banquet where she used her daughter Salome's appeal to Herod's lust to extract an oath from him to grant her any wish. Prompted by her mother, she asked for John's head. John was beheaded in the fortress prison Machaerus, east of the Dead Sea.

No less significant in this grisly story is the note that when Herod heard of Jesus' remarkable deeds, he thought it was John the Baptist all over again, either John risen from the dead or another prophet of the same ilk. Soon after this incident Jesus withdrew to a desert place.

He still had too much to do to risk John's fate at the hands of Herod.

Feeding the Five Thousand (14:13-21)

The fact that this episode appears in all four Gospels (Matthew 14:13-21; Mark 6:31-44; Luke 9:10-17; John 6:1-14), with duplicate stories in Mark and Matthew (Matthew 15:32-39; Mark 8:1-9), gives it a singular importance. But within the story itself we find striking symbolism of the Christian eucharist (thanksgiving over the bread when the Lord's Supper is memorialized). The elaborate significance of the event in the Fourth Gospel where John associates the feeding of the multitude with Jesus' words, *I am the bread of life* (John 6:35), leaves no doubt about the meaning which the early Christians saw in what happened in that lonely place. Indeed, John has no other account of anything that could be called the Lord's Supper.

The great messianic banquet that is to take place at the close of the age is a recurring theme in the teachings of Jesus. Clearly in this feeding of the multitude Jesus acts out that anticipated feast. Early Christians associated this gathering with the feast that was to come at the end-time. We cannot know in any detail what happened on that day. But what happened literally is less important than the meaning that the Gospel gives to the event. The words, *He looked up to heaven and blessed . . . and broke . . . and gave* echo the last Supper (NRSV, 26:26). Or perhaps the Last Supper echoes this feeding of the five thousand. We can suppose that Christians remembered some occasion when Jesus fed them in a special way and they went away satisfied in body because they had been filled in spirit. The twelve baskets full (one for each disciple) are a promise that Jesus always gives more than enough.

Jesus Walks on the Water (14:22-27)

People have speculated about this episode, even suggesting that it might be one of the post-Resurrection appearances transposed to Jesus' earthly lifetime. It has all the earmarks of the miracle stories told about many religious figures throughout history. As in the miraculous feeding, we can never know what happened literally. It is more important to see this as a symbol story or paradigm for the church, buffeted by winds and waves, and far from any safe harbor. This is the situation in which Christian disciples would always find themselves. In those days it would be a matter of life and death for the disciples to hear Jesus say, "Take heart, it is I." The people of Matthew's church would hear Jesus say those words to them through this story in the Gospel.

Peter's Little Faith (14:28-33)

The conclusion of the storm story is fascinating in what it tells us about the very human Peter, grandstanding before his fellow disciples, impulsive, self-assured, courageous, then suddenly frightened, finally crying desperately for help. The story also paints a vivid picture of the disciples in the times to come, needing the help of Jesus. With winds and waves against them none (not even Peter, a "half-believer") was self-sufficient.

It is unlikely that the words in verse 33 were uttered in this context. The great confession of Peter, *You are the Christ (Messiah)* (16:16) is the dramatic turning point of the Gospel. These words, *You are the Son of the living God*, were probably read back into this episode in the light of all that subsequently took place.

Jesus Heals Many (14:34-36)

Just as the feeding of the multitude and the affair on the turbulent sea had demonstrated Jesus' superhuman power, so now Matthew reports that for sick people to even touch Jesus' garment brought healing. These episodes set the stage for the revelations at Caesarea-Philippi (16:13-23) and the Transfiguration

(17:1-13), and provide a stunning contrast with the Pharisees in the next chapter.

Controversy Over Ritual Cleanliness (15:1-20)

The fact that these Pharisees came from Jerusalem tells us that criticism of Jesus had reached to the highest centers of Jewish authority.

Jesus does not condemn ritual cleanliness as such. The issue here is whether to put tradition above the law of God. The tradition was the accumulated interpretation of the written law made by priests over the years. The argument in this case is over whether a man who has pledged a gift to God (*Corban*, NIV, Mark 7:11) now has any further responsibility toward mother and father (the fifth commandment, Exodus 20:12). Jesus denounces any such evasion of responsibility under the commandments in favor of the tradition.

Jesus calls the people to hear his pronouncement that one is defiled, not by what is eaten, but by what comes out of the mouth. This statement sweeps away a whole system of reckoning what is clean (of being externally fastidious) in favor of inward purity and righteousness.

No wonder the Pharisees are offended. The legalisms by which they defined Jewish faithfulness are blown over by Jesus' words. These ritual requirements must never be honored above moral obedience and response to human need. Verse 14 has a ring of finality: *Let them alone* (NRSV; NIV = *Leave them*). Jesus comes close to a complete break with the Pharisees. When the report of his defiance reaches Jerusalem, Jesus' challenge will not go unanswered.

Jesus lists seven defiling vices that come out of the heart. Mark has thirteen transgressions (Mark 7:21-22), including *theft, murder, adultery, deceit, envy and folly.* Matthew has added *false witness testimony.*

Encounter with Gentiles (15:21-39)

The remainder of Chapter 15 holds a crucial place in the emergence of the Christian church. Gentiles are finding their way into the community of the followers of

Jesus. The response of the church to this mingling with non-Jews is symbolized by Jesus' response to Gentile people in the final three episodes of Chapter 15.

Tyre and Sidon (verse 21) are in the region now occupied by Lebanon on the Mediterranean coast.

Canaanite (verse 22) means a descendant of the people in Palestine before the Israelites entered at the end of the Exodus. Mark 7:26 identifies the woman as Greek because she spoke that language, but also as Syrophoenician, meaning that she came from Phoenicia. The central point lies in the facts that she was a Gentile, belonging to a people historically at enmity with Israel, and that the meeting occurred outside Israel and at her instigation.

The exchange between Jesus and the woman raises troublesome questions. Jesus already had met with great faith among the Gentiles (9:32-33), so why would he seem to put her off? He may want to emphasize that his mission is still first to the nation of Israel. As the conversation develops, Jesus' replies seem heartless: *It is not fair to take the children's food and throw it to the dogs* (NRSV, verse 26). Her quick retort, *Even the dogs eat the crumbs*, breaks through Jesus' testing of her faith and motivation. He says, *You have great faith* (NIV). Her daughter is instantly healed.

Jesus' power to heal caused such wonder among the Gentiles that they *praised the God of Israel* (verse 31). If the church in Matthew's day wondered about a mission to the Gentiles, here certainly was the charter.

The feeding of the *four thousand* differs from the *five thousand* (14:13-21) only in details. The important difference between the two stories lies in the people who shared the two meals. Presumably the multitude of four thousand was Gentile, whereas the five thousand were Jews. Jesus speaks the same words in each case. Fragments are gathered up to fill seven (not twelve) baskets, a significant number for Greeks. This feast for the four thousand is unique, for it symbolizes the inclusion of Gentiles in the church. Jesus blesses, breaks, and gives the bread for the whole world.

§ § § § § § §

The Message of Matthew 14–15

How did Jesus perform the miracle of feeding all those people? Was it superhuman power that simply multiplied the bread ten thousand times? Did people share what they had until all had enough? Did a small piece satisfy the hunger of each one because Jesus had broken the loaf? Matthew doesn't tell us. This we do know from nearly two thousand years of history: When Jesus breaks the bread of life to us we are more than satisfied. We are filled with new life, new purpose, new faith. This fulfillment is the continuing miracle.

To frightened, desperate souls, driven by overpowering winds and waves, Jesus somehow still speaks through the tumult. His presence inspires courage, quiets anxiety, gives assurance that whether we live or die we belong to God (Romans 14:8). For days and nights when the winds are against us, this story is a reminder that we are not alone.

At least Peter got out of the boat! When Jesus said, "Come," Peter jumped in the water. He had not reckoned on what it took to walk to Jesus on the water. Presumably he learned. Peter is a model of courage here, if not wisdom and faith.

Jesus' quotation in 15:9 waves a warning flag to us. How convenient it sometimes is to elevate our own self-interest to the level of a doctrine of God!

The nameless Canaanite woman should hold an honored place in the Christian church. She called out to Jesus for help and mercy. And although she was not of the covenant people, he answered her. Her voice still calls from outside our churches in the voices of people not part of the Christian community, but in great need of help, mercy, understanding, and faith.

§ § § § § § §

MATTHEW

Matthew 16–17

Introduction to This Chapter

From the mountain of the temptations (chapter 4) to
the Sermon on the Mount (chapters 5–7) to the mountain
of the Great Commission (chapter 28), the highest
moments of Matthew's Gospel are associated with the
highest places. In chapter 17 we ascend with Jesus, Peter,
James, and John to another peak of towering importance:
the Transfiguration. The epiphany that occurs on that
mountain, and Peter's confession of faith that precedes it
(chapter 16), mark a decisive turning point in the life and
mission of Jesus. These two events provide a key to the
central meaning and purpose of the Gospel: the
forthright and forceful declaration that Jesus is the
Christ, and his validation as God's beloved Son.

These two chapters conclude the narrative part of
Matthew's section four on the church. Through the
events that happen here Jesus teaches his disciples what
it will mean to be an apostle and to minister in the
church. They are with him in controversy with the
Pharisees and Sadducees learning to beware of the
corrupting leaven of their teaching. After Peter's
confession, Jesus tells his disciples that he will suffer
many things from the elders and chief priests and will be
killed. When Peter protests this announcement, Jesus
rebukes him as a man who speaks for Satan. The
disciples are told that they too must take up the same
cross as Jesus. In discovering that they cannot heal an

epileptic boy, the disciples learn that healing requires more than a little faith. Finally Jesus teaches the need to compromise sometimes in order not to give offense. We can say in all truth that this chapter represents "field education" for the disciples.

Here is an outline of chapters 16–17.

Warning of Pharisees and Sadducees (16:1-12)

Verses 1-4 appear to repeat 12:38-39, except that Matthew brings the Sadducees into the controversy here. They were bitter enemies of the Pharisees. The parties disagreed about nearly everything—the resurrection, the messiah, the law. But they both wanted Jesus out of the way. Their demand for a sign was not an act of faith. It was to test (tempt) Jesus. (Recall 4:5-7.) Matthew also introduces the metaphor of the "weather signs," appearance of the sky but not the signs of the times.

But Matthew has a further purpose for placing this conflict at this point. We might identify this confrontation as "teaching by the case method." The disciples were learning firsthand that they needed to beware of the leaven of the Pharisees. Everywhere in the New Testament, except Matthew 13:33, yeast is a metaphor for evil and debasing influence. The disciples are warned by this figure of speech that the teaching of the two religious parties is an evil corruption of the faith of Israel. In this curious exchange the disciples completely misunderstand what Jesus is talking about. They think he refers to their failure to bring real bread.

As on numerous other occasions, Jesus must painfully spell out for them what he means. The point is not an incidental one. The church in Matthew's time needed particularly to beware of the teaching of the Jerusalem Pharisees which would corrupt the true faith in Jesus as the Son of God.

Peter's Confession of Faith (16:13-28)

The remaining sixteen verses of this chapter have a unity of purpose easily overlooked as we consider closely each of the four parts: verses 13-16, 17-20, 21-23, and 24-28. Matthew has used the original account of the event as it appears in Mark 8:27–9:1. But he has added material to serve the later purpose of his Gospel. Some of his additions reflect more of a post-Resurrection faith than what might have been said at the time. We will first sketch the overall intention of Matthew's design and then consider some details of his account.

Matthew wants it understood that Jesus is the Christ, the chosen one of God. He is the one for whom all others were forerunners, especially Elijah and John the Baptist (verses 14-16). Such a claim is made on the basis not of logic but of a direct revelation from God (verse 17). It must be clear, however, that Jesus fits no traditional expectation of the messiah; he will suffer at the hands of the elders and chief priests and be killed. However, he will be raised by God from the dead (verse 21).

Because of these things the followers of Jesus will make their life together in the church bearing the name of Jesus (verse 18). To Peter will be given authority to make both temporal and eternal judgments (verse 19). These things will come to pass even before all the disciples have died (verse 28).

Such a scenario clearly fits the situation for which Matthew prepared his Gospel. We may consider it unlikely that Jesus foresaw a "Christian" church, bearing his name and separated from Israel. But by the time

Matthew wrote, that separation was taking place. The new wine of the gospel had burst the old wineskins of the institutions of Israel. Even if Jesus did recognize himself as God's Messiah, he wanted no such announcement to be made. People would not only misunderstand the kind of messiah Jesus asserted himself to be, but the opposition would have silenced him immediately. Instead he commanded secrecy from the disciples, and warned them and all who came after them that they too would suffer, even as he had.

Caesarea-Philippi was a pagan city named by Herod's son Philip in honor of one of the Caesars and of himself. It was located among the fertile sources of the Jordan River on the southwestern slope of Mount Hermon. It is ironic that this city, where tradition places Peter's definitive confession of Christian faith, was the site of an ancient shrine to Pan, the Greek god of fertility and flocks.

Matthew adds to the original account *the Son of the living God* (verse 16) in order to make clear that Jesus is more than a divinely anointed king of Israel, which is what the term *Christ* meant in Jewish messianic hope.

Only in Matthew do we read of Jesus' response to Peter's confession. No other words of Jesus have provoked such partisan debate as these! Upon them the Roman Catholic Church has based its structure of the ecclesiastical hierarchy deriving from the "primacy of Peter." Most non-Roman scholars understand these words to indicate Peter as the first witness of the Resurrection and therefore as the prime apostolic witness that God raised Jesus from the dead.

Away from me, Satan recalls the temptation of Jesus (NIV, 4:10). Here Peter speaks for Satan in trying to distract Jesus from the way of the cross.

We note that Jesus speaks of the Son of Man in the third person: *the Son of Man is to come*, NRSV. Possibly Jesus did not identify himself with the apocalyptic judge of the end time. Whatever title he may have used to identify himself, Jesus believed that he had a vocation from God unlike that of any other person.

The Transfiguration (17:1-13)

This transfiguration occurs immediately following the confession that Jesus is the Christ and his prediction of his suffering and death. It marks a decisive turning point in the life of Jesus, away from Galilee and toward the Passion in Jerusalem. And it bears a remarkable resemblance to the epiphany that Moses experienced in the Exodus. For all of these reasons, no question remains that the Transfiguration has key importance in the Christian story, giving higher place only to the Crucifixion and Resurrection.

Transfiguration means literally the change in appearance of a person, scene, or event, so that whoever is witness recognizes a truth and reality beyond the ordinary appearance. On the mountain Jesus appears in a glory of which the disciples had not been aware.

As in Exodus 24:9-18, where Moses ascends the mountain with three companions, Jesus takes with him Peter, James, and John. Mount Hermon, rising as it does above Caesarea-Philippi, is the most likely setting for this episode. However it may have happened, the disciples suddenly see Jesus as a heavenly being whose *face shone like the sun.* The three disciples unexpectedly find themselves witness to an epiphany—a showing forth of the utmost significance. This importance is confirmed by the appearance of Moses and Elijah, representing the Law and the Prophets. Both of these men were believed to have been translated to heaven. For Jesus to be talking with them is an unmistakable sign of his own divine connection.

Peter likes what he sees here much more than what he heard at Caesarea-Philippi. He suggests that he make three booths where all the heavenly figures can remain (until the end time?). The feast of Tabernacles (Booths) was associated with Israel's first place among the nations in the age to come. Obviously Peter has not yet understood that Jesus will be glorified *through* suffering and death, not *instead of* them. Peter embraces the tradition of Elijah coming in glory before the Son of man appears, while Jesus identifies with the suffering servant of Isaiah.

As in the Mount Sinai revelation (Exodus 24:16), God speaks out of a bright cloud. The words are the same as those spoken at Jesus' baptism (3:17).

Jesus tells the inquiring disciples (16:10-11) that Elijah has already come, meaning in the person of John the Baptist. What they (Herod and the elders of the people) did to John they will do also to Jesus.

We remember the appalling scene that greeted Moses as he came down from Mount Sinai (the golden calf, Exodus 32). Jesus' patience is tested here. To the disciples he had given power to heal, and because of their little faith they had failed. Verse 20 can unsettle the faith of anyone who reads it as a promise that with faith a person can do anything he or she wishes. Such promises are given in the context of doing the will and work of Jesus: *I will do whatever you ask in my name* (John 14:13).

Second Prediction of the Passion (17:22-23)

For the second time Jesus predicts his passion and death (also in 16:21 and 20:17-19). Matthew softens Mark's bluntness: *But they did not understand what he meant, and they were afraid to ask him about it* (Mark 9:32). Taking his cue from Jesus himself, Matthew gives no one a chance to imagine that passion, suffering, and death can be bypassed by the glory of the Transfiguration.

The Temple Tax (17:24-27)

It would be a great loss if we allowed the principal purpose of this story to pass unnoticed in the wonder of the fable to which it is attached. Nothing in the Gospels leads us to make of Jesus a magician or soothsayer, able to see or know under the water which fish had a coin in its mouth, and able to cause that fish to be hooked by Peter. That would be wizardry, and Jesus was not a wizard!

The story has to do with Christian freedom. Although Christians are free from Jewish law, they must not use their freedom in a way to give offense (cause others to stumble). Paul meets this issue head-on in 1 Corinthians 8:8-13. Prior to A.D. 70 the Romans collected a tax from all Jews to maintain the Temple in Jerusalem. When the Temple was destroyed, the Romans continued to levy the tax in support of the shrine of Jupiter erected where the Temple had once stood. Apparently Jesus is saying: You have no obligation to pay such a tax for purposes of idolatry. But you do have an obligation not to give cause for any others to stumble. (Especially in Matthew's time beneficiaries of freedom in Christ would need to remember their Jewish brothers and sisters still under the law.) Idolatry is prohibited. But maybe on this issue Jesus chose not to challenge the state.

§ § § § § § §

The Message of Matthew 11–12

"Who do you say that I am?" Jesus asked Peter.
Supposedly you know me best. Who am I? Matthew,
through his Gospel, sends Jesus' question down the
corridors of history to our time and place. Who do *we* say
that Jesus is? As far as our lives are concerned this is the
ultimate question. It does make a difference whether we
say that Jesus is one whom we can trust with our sin
when we need forgiveness, whose light we can follow in
darkness, in whose word we can find comfort when life
tumbles in. Blessed are we when we can say: "Jesus is the
Christ, Son of the living God!"

What are we putting on the scale to "balance" God's
gift of life? Acquisitions, popularity, insulation from the
world's pain, the cries of the hungry, the lonely, the
desperate, insurance that we will never lose our life for
anyone or anything but ourselves? Or are we willing to
give up these things if only we could be given back our
souls, our freedom to love God and neighbors?

Moments of transfiguration have come to most people
when they have seen the surpassing wonder and glory of
life. We treasure such "mountaintop experiences." But it
is not given to us to live in some mountaintop tabernacle.
There is a world down below suffering demonic seizures
of every kind. To this world we are called in Christ's
name to descend and meet the real test of our faith.

There can be no healing, whether of physical, moral,
emotional, or spiritual distress, without faith. Faith alone
may not move a mountain to yonder place. But without
faith in a power that gives life, nothing will move.

§ § § § § § §

PART TEN Matthew 18

Introduction to This Chapter

From the narrative in chapters 14–17 it is clear that the followers of Christ have been set free from obedience to the Pharisaic law of Israel. But unless their lives are gathered together under some kind of disciplined order and control, moral and spiritual anarchy will be the fruits of their freedom. So Matthew gathers a group of the sayings of Jesus into a manual of church discipline.

Chapter 18 forms the teaching discourse of section four in the Gospel of Matthew. Originally these sayings were addressed to the disciples. Matthew has assembled them as instructions to the leaders of the apostolic church emerging in Matthew's time, late in the first century.

Looking at this chapter as a whole, we discern seven distinguishing marks of the life of a congregation:
1. Living together in humility toward one another (18:4)
2. Seeing the Christ in one another (18:5)
3. Living so as to give no offense to anyone (18:7)
4. Caring for the weak little ones (18:10)
5. Accepting moral/spiritual discipline by the church (18:17)
6. Praying together in the congregation (18:20)
7. Forgiving one another without limit (18:21-22)

The central theme of the chapter is: Who is the greatest in the kingdom of heaven?

Here is an outline of chapter 18.

Humble Yourself Like a Child (18:1-4)

Humility is the first mark of the Christian disciple in the church. To illustrate this point, Jesus sets a child in the midst of the disciples. He points to the characteristic humility of a young child as model for how a follower of Jesus is to make himself (herself) worthy of the Kingdom. Matthew omits the unbecoming account of the disciples wondering who would be greatest in the Kingdom (Mark 9:33-34). In Matthew the disciples ask Jesus the general question, *Who is the greatest?*

Whoever Receives a Child (18:5-6)

In Matthew 25:31-46 we will come upon the fullest exposition of this theme: to receive a little one in Jesus' name is to receive him. Here in verses 5-6 we have a variant of Luke 10:16. *Little one* is not an exclusive reference to children. In verses 6, 10, and 14 the text has in mind the members new to the faith and fellowship of Jesus' followers. Such newcomers needed unusually solicitous care. Some were Jews living for the first time without the anchor of the Jewish law; some were Greeks to whom the whole religion was new.

Woe to Those Who Tempt Others (18:7-9)

Jesus here reminds us that our actions can sometimes appeal to a weakness that another person cannot control. We distinguish this from deliberate temptation. This is a matter of sensitivity to the susceptibility of another person to occasions for sin, or for them to lose their faith in Christ. (See below, "The Message of Matthew 18.") Verses 8-9 are hyperbole; they are extreme exaggeration to emphasize how urgent *encouraging* behavior really is. The *valley of Gehenna* was the place where the refuse of Jerusalem was burned. It became the image for the "hell of fire" (NRSV; NIV = *fire of hell*, verse 9) expected at the close of the age for all who would not serve the Lord.

Care for the Little Ones (18:10-14)

Despise (*look down on*) means to treat with contempt. Verse 10 expresses a belief that the least important have representatives in the heavenly realms. These representatives look after the little ones in need of care and are able to intercede with God. The conclusion is that it would be better not to offend a little one whose angel has access to God!

Christians are to care for all of God's children, treating none with contempt. In the original source the parable that begins with verse 12 made the point that God cares for all lost persons. Matthew uses the parable as a way of making the church leaders aware of their responsibility for the least important members of the flock. One insignificant little one matters as much to God as ninety-nine stronger followers.

Yield to Church Discipline (18:15-19)

In these verses we see the beginning of a structure of church order and judicial procedure against various forms of misconduct in the church. We can even recognize a primitive form of excommunication, which was to be such a terrifying weapon in later history. Verse 18 refers to Peter's appointment as custodian of the keys of heaven and hell. In this manual of church discipline the disciples, as a cadre or band of leaders, are all apparently to exercise powers of judgment. Peter was not the only one with this responsibility.

Gather in Jesus' Name (18:20)

In effect Jesus promises here what he will later pledge at the close of the Gospel in the Great Commission (28:20): that he will be in the midst of a praying church. What seems like an unconditional promise is qualified by the condition *in my name* (see "The Message of Matthew 18" below).

Forgive Seventy Times Seven (18:21-35)

Jesus' answer to Peter's questions, *seventy seven times* (verse 22), and the contrast between ten thousand talents (verse 24) and one hundred denarii (verse 28) push the command to forgive the wayward one and backslider beyond all limits. Ten thousand talents converts into ten million dollars; a hundred denarii equals about twenty dollars. The inequality of our refusal to forgive a trifling offense compared to God's enormous forgiveness of our sin becomes ludicrous. Such forceful teaching of the church leaders was an attempt to put an end to bickering and retaliation for offenses between members. Such settling of personal "scores" pales into shameful pettiness when measured by God's limitless love even for gross offenders.

§ § § § § § §

The Message of Matthew 18

What Matthew wanted church leaders to understand, church members today still need to recognize. How often is one person's behavior an inducement to someone else to follow suit and find himself or herself in trouble? Sensitivity to the weakness and capabilities of other persons is still required for all Christians. Woe to the person who takes sensitivity lightly!

Jesus told us when we pray to go into our room and shut the door (6:6). Private, solitary prayer brings us close to God. But when two or three are gathered in Christ's name to pray, each gives his or her private agenda to all the others, and receives from them enlargement of personal view and correction of selfish direction. People are created for community. And the heart and soul of Christian community is common prayer.

How do we despise each other? We belittle someone else's effort and achievement. We put people down with derogatory comments about their face, nationality, or religion. We spread rumors and innuendos about another's behavior. We despise persons by our cold indifference to anything they do. We make them feel like nothing, worthless. We confirm in their minds what they already feel about themselves: They are insignificant. Jesus spoke a word in season about all of this: See that you do not treat one of the common people with contempt.

How can we go on forgiving and forgiving those who continue to hurt and destroy? Sentimentality is the enemy of true Christian love. Social order requires restraint. But through it all we can and will forgive because we remember how much God has forgiven us.

§ § § § § § §

Matthew 19–20

Introduction to These Chapters

Section five of the Gospel of Matthew (chapters 19–25) is commonly called *The Judgment;* in it Matthew includes much of what Jesus said about the judgment to come at the end of the age. Chapters 19–23 are narrative, with teaching units added in association with events that were happening to Jesus and the disciples. Chapters 24–25 are the teaching discourse on judgment.

We have no way of knowing for sure the exact order of events in Jesus' life, nor when he said the things that the Gospels report. But the record is clear that following the episodes at Caesarea-Philippi and the Transfiguration Jesus moved his ministry from Galilee to Judea, beginning his journey to Jerusalem. Chapters 19–25 give us the clear sense of increasingly bitter conflict between Jesus and the Jerusalem authorities. The menacing shadow of the cross draws closer and closer.

In chapter 19 the Pharisees first confront Jesus with a loaded question about divorce, hoping to confound him in answers contradictory to the law. The final fourteen verses speak about riches and the kingdom of heaven, turning upside down the priorities that people customarily honor.

The longest unit in chapter 20 is a parable about laborers in the vineyard, with its uncomfortable disclosure that the economy of God's grace has an entirely different design from the ways by which we usually order our lives. After a third prediction of the

Passion, the narrative shifts to a discussion of greatness in the Kingdom in which the disciples once again show themselves to be slow learners. Finally we have the incident of Jesus' healing two blind men in Jericho. This brings us to the eve of Jesus' entrance into Jerusalem.

Here is an outline of chapters 19–20.

I. Jesus Enters Judea (19:1-2)
II. Marriage, Divorce, and Celibacy (19:3-12)
III. Blessing the Children (19:13-15)
IV. Riches and Possessions (19:16-30)
   A. A young man's questions (19:16-22)
   B. Jesus talks about rewards (19:23-30)
V. Parable of the Vineyard (20:1-16)
VI. The Crucifixion and Resurrection (20:17-19)
VII. Jesus' Teaching About Greatness (20:20-28)
VIII. Jesus Heals Two Blind Men (20:29-34)

Jesus Enters Judea (19:1-2)

When Jesus enters Judea, he moves from friendly soil to "enemy territory." In present-day athletics we say we lose the home-field advantage when games are played on opponents' fields. The opposition which was to crucify Jesus was centered in Judea. (See the map on page 160.)

Marriage, Divorce, and Celibacy (19:3-12)

The implications of these words for Christians today are discussed under "The Message of Matthew 19-20."

These verses from Matthew must be compared with Mark 10:1-12, Luke 16:18, and 1 Corinthians 7:10. Those passages almost certainly reflect what Jesus said about divorce. *Except for unchastity* (NRSV; NIV = *marital unfaithfulness* found also in 5:32) was added by Matthew as a way of accommodating to the situation among Christians for whom the Gospel was prepared. Obviously the Pharisees jumped at the chance to quote Deuteronomy 24:1-4, where Moses seems to permit divorce for some indecency, meaning unchastity (NIV) or because the husband found *something objectionable* about the wife (NRSV). Jesus avoids this trap by taking his stand on Genesis 1:27 and 2:24: *A man will leave his father and mother and be united to his wife, and they will become one flesh* (NIV). Marriage is the expression of this understanding, and shall not be undone by anyone or anything.

Jesus acknowledges that for peoples' *hardness of heart* (their stubbornness) Moses relaxed the restriction. But it was never that way from the beginning of creation. And just as Moses had to compromise with human reality, so the early Christians had to come to terms with both the perfect will of God and the weakness of human nature.

Jesus does not advocate celibacy (verses 10-12) as a possible alternative to marriage for all Christians. Celibacy is a gift only for those who can receive it, and not superior to marriage. The discussion contains no hint of the idea that only celibates can be ministers in the church. But the saying in verse 12 reflects an attitude already appearing in the first century that celibacy is a superior condition of holiness.

Blessing the Children (19:13-15)

We wrongly associate these verses with baptism. Jesus did not baptize, and the verses here have no sacramental meaning in the sense that we now understand sacraments in the church. They do relate to baptism in the sense that children are important in the company of the church. Those who do not receive them as such do not belong to the kingdom of heaven.

A Young Man's Question (19:16-22)

In Mark the young man who comes to Jesus calls him *good teacher*. Matthew shifts the adjective *good* from *teacher* to *deed (thing)*. By so doing no comparison is suggested between the goodness of Jesus and the goodness of God. It seems as though the man is bargaining with Jesus; *which ones* sound childish, as though some of them didn't matter. When he boasts that he has kept all of these, he may be expecting a pat on the back. Instead Jesus lays upon him the challenge of complete divestiture of his possessions.

Perfect (verse 21) conjures up the idea of moral perfection, as though by deeds one can run up a perfect score for admission to eternal life. A better understanding may be gained by the word *true:* if you would be *true* to God. The man didn't want to go that far!

Jesus Talks About Rewards (19:23-30)

The disciples are unusually perceptive in their astonishment (verse 25). Wealth cannot save anyone. But Peter, who always seems to want to avoid the difficult choices, immediately asks, in effect: "What's in it for us?" Jesus' answer, however, is not to criticize but to encourage. Suffering and persecution await the disciples. They are not to lose heart, for in the new world great will be the reward for their faithfulness.

Parable of the Vineyard (20:1-16)

All kinds of difficulties attend this parable when we try to read it as a lesson for our economic life or social order. This is a parable not about work and wages, but about God's grace and generosity. What better way than through the illustration of "equal pay for unequal work" could Jesus have chosen to write large the truth that one does not, and cannot, earn God's grace by long hours and good work. Grace overflows from God's generosity. We do not receive it in proportion to our merit, but in the measure of God's unconditional love. (See "The Message of Matthew 19-20.")

Only with the first group does the householder make contractual agreement. The others are told, or they assume, that they will be paid *whatever is right.*

The parable makes no point of why the eleventh-hour workers had not been hired. That is irrelevant.

The only significance to the order of payment is to set up the surprise climax.

The ones who worked twelve hours had good reason to protest the inequality of the pay scale. Are they to have no added bonus for their toil through hours of scorching heat?

A denarius was a most generous day's wage. For that alone they had no basis for complaint; only when they learned that the one-hour workers (in the cool of the afternoon, at that!) received the same did they feel exploited. So their grumbling is not at the agreement they made, but at someone else's equal benefit.

The parable makes one point, and all other details are extraneous. God gives of divine grace to all the disciples without distinction.

This parable casts its light for the disciples, for the elders of the people in Israel, and for Christians in the future. The disciples have worked and traveled with Jesus from the beginning; that will not entitle them to any more grace than the thief on the cross next to Jesus. The people of Israel, inheritors of the covenant made through Moses, will not receive greater preference than non-Jews who come lately. The grace of God is free to all, not dispensed according to any order of merit.

This parable appears only in Matthew.

The statement in verse 16 (repeated in verse order from 19:30) has been added to the original parable because it is related to the surprising end of the story.

Crucifixion and Resurrection (20:17-19)

Once again Jesus reminds his disciples how events will turn out in Jerusalem. It is a necessary word for the disciples to hear just before the triumphal entry (and to remember after the Resurrection).

Jesus' Teaching About Greatness (20:20-28)

In Mark 10:35-41 the two sons of Zebedee speak for themselves asking for the chief seats. Matthew senses that this is bad form, and gives the immodest question to their mother. Notice, however, that Jesus directs his answer to James and John.

Jesus' understanding of greatness contrasts 180 degrees from the way the *rulers of the Gentiles* perceive it. But *greatness* had to be transformed even within Israel.

Isaiah 53:11-12 provides Jesus with a model for what the Son of man will be, the suffering servant who gives his life to bear *the sin of many. Ransom* in this passage signifies no particular theory of the atonement. The text simply announces that the death of Jesus will have the profound effect of releasing people from slavery to sin.

Jesus Heals Two Blind Men (20:29-34)

These two blind men twice cry out to Jesus as *Son of David*, expressing the messianic hope that David's kingdom will be restored. They also address him as *Lord*, a title by which Christians will acclaim him after the Resurrection. On his way up to the Holy City where he will die, Jesus still has eyes for little ones who suffer, and he touches their eyes with the gift of sight.

§ § § § § § §

The Message of Matthew 19–20

Whoever divorces his wife, except for unchastity (marital unfaithfulness), and marries another, commits adultery (19:9). This is a hard saying. It has caused heartache and guilt across the centuries. And it deeply divides the church today. Roughly one out of every two marriages in the United States ends in divorce. And not for unchastity alone. Divorce on the grounds of irreconcilable differences is now granted in most places. Many Christian marriages end in divorce, Matthew 19:9 notwithstanding. What does the passage say to us?

Marriage is a sacred covenant, "till death us do part." It is not to be entered into casually, nor put off lightly. But we are human, with a human nature that overrides the marriage covenant not only by sexual adultery but by selfishness and insensitivity as well. Where this happens people often acknowledge their failure and infidelity, but conclude that continuing a loveless and destructive marriage is a sin greater than divorce. God forgives sin, even the sin of adultery. Jesus said to one taken in adultery, *"Go your way, and from now on do not sin again"* (NRSV, John 8:11).

Such argument offers no invitation to take marriage less seriously, or to rationalize our way out of failure. The bond between husband and wife is still the most sacred of all human commitments. Each has to decide how he or she can honor it best.

By the most common lines of human reason, for the householder to pay his laborers as he did is absurd, just as it would be absurd to so disperse a payroll in any company today. But the parable is not really about work and wages. It is an uncommonly effective way of getting our attention, and letting us know that in the economy of God's grace no one earns any more than another.

Symbolically speaking, twelve hours of work do not earn any more than one hour. To the thief on the cross (Luke 23:39-43) and the woman who anointed Jesus' feet (Luke 7:37-38) Jesus gave the same full measure that he gave to Peter, James, and John.

Two blind men cried out to Jesus as Lord. These two men suffered no impairment of their spiritual vision. In fact they saw what a 20-20 vision missed: that one was passing by who could give them sight. They followed Jesus up the road and presumably into the city where sighted people were "blind." They were blind to what God had given them to see by faith. Faith has the power to see what sight may withhold. These two nameless men (Mark calls the blind man in his account *Bartimaeus*) remind us that our greatest handicap may be looking without seeing. *Let our eyes be opened.*

§ § § § § § §

Matthew 21–23

Introduction to These Chapters

Chapters 21–23 continue the narrative portion of the fifth section of the Gospel According to Matthew. They contain the reports of eleven events or confrontations that occurred in Jerusalem during the week that ended with the death of Jesus on the cross. Matthew wants to show how the conflict between Jesus and the authorities led to the Crucifixion. He needs also to encourage the leaders of the early Christian church as they face the same conflict with the Jerusalem authorities of Matthew's time.

We read here the story of the triumphal entry into Jerusalem, followed by the episodes of the cleansing of the Temple and Jesus' healing in that sacred place. The authorities (scribes, Pharisees, Sadducees) precipitate three controversies with Jesus—over Jesus' authority, the poll tax, and resurrection. Jesus provokes a fourth dispute over messiahship and the Son of David. Jesus tells two parables that condemn the leaders of Israel—the two sons and the rejected invitation to the marriage feast. We also find an elaborate allegory here—the story of the wicked tenants—which a later editor has created from a parable of Jesus.

The final verses of chapter 21 are the first report of an actual conspiracy to destroy Jesus. The most bitter and scathing denunciation of the scribes in all the Gospels makes up the greater part of chapter 23, with the seven woes, which condemn these leaders as hypocrites.

Here is an outline of chapters 21–23.

The Triumphal Entry (21:1-11)

Of all the events in the public ministry of Jesus, only the trial and Crucifixion are more remembered and celebrated than the triumphal entry into Jerusalem. All four Gospels draw upon the Old Testament prophecy of Zechariah 9:9 of Israel's king coming to the Holy City *riding on a donkey, on a colt the foal of a donkey.* We cannot believe that Jesus rode two animals into Jerusalem like a circus acrobat. Zechariah has two animals and Matthew copies him literally. The tradition understands this pageant to be symbolic speech announcing Jesus as king, Messiah, Son of David. Other details give further support to the fulfillment motif of Matthew's account (see 2 Kings 9:13). To what extent Jesus intentionally proclaimed himself Messiah it is impossible to know. Such a story, we suspect, would be overlaid after the fact by the faith that arose with the Resurrection.

Hosanna means *save now.* Such a cry reveals the surging

hope among many that Jesus would deliver Israel from pagan rulers (Isaiah 62:11; Psalm 118:25-26).

Blessed is he . . . would have been asked for all pilgrims to Jerusalem. Matthew makes it a particular supplication for Jesus.

Driving Out the Money Changers (21:12-17)

Matthew states that Jesus went immediately to the Temple and drove out the money changers in the outer court. Matthew sees this incident as fulfillment of Isaiah 56:7 and Jeremiah 7:11. The priests controlled the whole sacrificial system; they changed outrageous prices for the only pigeons considered acceptable for sacrifice. A portion of this lucrative income the priests pocketed for themselves. In overturning the tables of these priestly bandits exploiting the poor, Jesus disturbed a source of enormous profit and graft in the Temple. As if this were not enough, the children crying their hosannas in these sacred precincts offended the priests. That Jesus accepted their accolades was blasphemy.

Jesus Curses a Fig Tree (21:18-22)

Why would Jesus blast this fruitless fig tree? We can scarcely make sense of this story, so out of character for Jesus, unless we read it symbolically. Israel is expected to bear the fruits of repentance. Because the nation fails to produce such fruit, God will wither the tree. Verses 21-22 are an affirmation of faith in prayer; they have little to do with the symbolic meaning of the fig tree. It may be that this episode is a dramatized acting-out of a parable in Luke 13:6-9.

Question About Jesus' Authority (21:23-27)

Only those ordained as rabbis could act with authority in the Temple. Jesus had no such credentials. But instead of giving a self-incriminating answer to the authority question (verse 23), Jesus asks the priest an embarrassing question about the authority of John the Baptist. The chief priests cannot say that John's authority was from God without condemning themselves; they did not receive John as God's prophet. They cannot say that John had no authority from God because he had been acclaimed a prophet by the people. They refuse to answer; Jesus refuses to answer them.

Two Parables (21:28-44)

These two parables with their stinging rebuke of the religious leaders of Israel naturally infuriate the priests. In the first story Jesus denounces them as ones who make a pretense of faith. They say yes, but never translate it into deeds or moral obedience to God. The tax collectors and harlots, sinners and non-Jews make no claim to be holy. They do not say yes, but they respond in faith to Jesus.

After hearing the second story, the parable of the wicked tenants, the chief priests and the elders condemn themselves in their reply to Jesus' question (verse 41). Not until Jesus interprets the story in the light of Psalm 118:22-23 do the leaders realize that Jesus has told the story against *them*, that *they* are the wicked tenants, and that God has taken the kingdom away from them. Of course, they immediately conspire to do away with Jesus.

This parable suited well the situation of the early Christian church, remembering the passion and death of the Son, and finding themselves once again in the same conflict with the authorities in Israel. The allegory as it now stands in Matthew is the perfect retrospective commentary on what happened to Jesus, and what still happens when those charged to perpetuate the faith and covenant reject the epiphanies and incarnations of God.

The Plot Against Jesus (21:45-46)

Had it not been for the crowds, the authorities would have arrested Jesus then and there. Jesus must have known that the high drama of trial and Crucifixion would serve God's purposes far better.

The Rejected Invitation (22:1-14)

Once more the behavior of the leaders is compared unfavorably with the response even of people from "the street corners" (non-Jews). Matthew changes the parallel parable in Luke 14:16-24, making it a king's wedding feast for his son. The wedding feast is a metaphor for the messianic banquet to which God will invite the faithful at the close of the age. The invited guests (the leaders of Israel) would not respond in faith to Jesus; they continued to go about their business as usual. So to take their places the king (God) called in "outsiders," Gentiles and others who were held in disrespect. In verse 10 we find a familiar note in this Gospel: both good and bad in the church whom God will judge at the end time.

Verses 6-7 seem to be a clear reference to the destruction of Jerusalem by the Romans in A.D. 70. It was not unprecedented among biblical writers to believe that God would use the power of Israel's enemy to punish unfaithfulness (see Isaiah 10:5).

The strange epilogue that Matthew adds (verses 11-14) shows that one can only come to the banquet of the Messiah clothed in the garments of righteousness. It was the custom of the time of the Gospel for a host to provide proper attire for all guests. The guest wearing no wedding garment had no excuse, even as the leaders of Israel had no excuse. God had sent Jesus to them, and they had made light of him.

Payment of Taxes to Caesar (22:15-22)

Three things are important to note about this episode. First is the unlikely conspiracy between the Herodians and the Pharisees. The Herodians supported Herod Antipas, a puppet ruler under Rome. To them, payment of the head tax of one denarius was the patriotic duty of every Roman subject. The Pharisees, by contrast, believed that to pay a tax to pagans who occupied "the holy land" of Israel was idolatry. But Herodians and Pharisees made common cause to incriminate Jesus.

The question (verse 17) was cleverly conceived. No matter what answer Jesus gave, he would condemn himself either as subversive of Roman law and order or unfaithful to Jewish commandment. Jesus' answer put the decision back upon his questioners. Persons had to decide what their faith and loyalty required them to do. Thus Jesus avoided a trap and left the ethical question to personal decision.

Controversy Over Resurrection (22:23-33)

In the previous controversy Jesus faced an alliance of Herodians and Pharisees. Here he finds another implausible affiliation of Sadducees and Pharisees. The Sadducees, who were the priestly party, held to the first five books of the Law (Genesis–Deuteronomy) as the primary law of Israel. Everything else was derivative. The Pharisees appealed to accumulated oral tradition and continuing interpretation of the Mosaic law. The Sadducees did not believe in the general resurrection; it was not part of the written law of Moses. The Pharisees did believe in resurrection. The question asked of Jesus was based on the Jewish law of levirate marriage, which required a man to marry his brother's widow (Deuteronomy 25:5) in order to ensure a son in the family. Jesus, of course, declares that in the resurrection the laws and order of this world will no longer be needed.

We do not know what *angels in heaven* are like. It is sufficient to know that there will be a life to meet whatever needs people may have. Jesus appeals to God as the God of Abraham, Isaac, and Jacob, who are still alive with God. The faithful will live with them.

The Greatest Commandment (22:34-40)

Jesus is not the first person to sum up the Jewish law in a condensed capsule. (See Psalm 15:2-5; Isaiah 33:15; Amos 5:4; Micah 6:8.) Such summarizing was also a

favorite device of the rabbis. The laws were not new with
Jesus. But the substance of what it means to love God and
who the neighbor is that one is to love—these bear his
unmistakable mark.

The Son of David (22:41-46)

The final controversy in this chapter Jesus initiates
himself. He asks the Pharisees, "Whose son is the
Christ?" (not the biological son, but his royal and
spiritual forebear). The best-known messianic Psalm,
110:1, is now quoted. Then Jesus says, "How can David
call one who is his son, his Lord?" Jesus seems here to
deny his lineage from David. Not really so. Jesus'
purpose is not to deny his historic ancestry, but to affirm
his sonship to God. He is saying that he is infinitely more
than a savior who will liberate Israel from Rome.

Warnings About the Pharisees (23:1-12)

Beginning back in chapter 9, the Gospel of Matthew
has been a long chronicle of controversy between Jesus
and the leaders of Israel. With chapter 23 we cross a
bridge from conflict to condemnation. This chapter, while
not formally a part of the teaching discourse on judgment
(chapters 24–25), sounds a severe verdict of judgment
upon the authorities. The first part condemns the
religious practices and behavior of the scribes and
Pharisees. The remainder of the chapter catalogues a
series of seven bitter woes called down on these
authorities. In the two final verses Jesus utters a tragic
lament over Jerusalem.

It is important to keep two things in mind at this point:
(1) Jesus does not condemn the Jewish law, and (2) Jesus
does not attack the Jewish nation or faith. It is the
hypocrisy of the scribes and Pharisees against which he
sounds judgment. There are sins that have been common
to all religious establishments and peoples, including the
Christians (see discussion above under 6:18).

They do not practice what they preach. (NIV, verse 3). Jesus orders his disciples to obey the law of Moses, which the Pharisees preach from the seat of authority in the synagogues. But do not do what they do! Jesus warns.

Heavy burdens (loads) (verse 4) refers to ceremonial law, enormously elaborated by commentary since Moses' day with rules so numerous and onerous that most people could not comply.

Jesus delivers his most bitter judgment against public pretense in the practice of piety. *Phylacteries* were amulets containing the commands of Exodus 13:16 and Deuteronomy 6:8 and 11:18. Unnecessarily broad phylacteries were worn conspicuously to be seen by others.

Rabbi (verse 8) can mean *my great one or my Lord,* but it more typically means *teacher* or *sir.* This injunction probably comes from the time after Jesus as a warning to Christian teachers not to assume any pretentious titles; all are to be equal in their vocation. *Rabbi* was not a title widely used in Jesus' day.

The aphorism of verse 12 is an expansion of 18:4 and contrasts Pharisaism with humility.

Seven Woes Against the Pharisees (23:13-36)

These seven woes form a catalogue of frightful transgressions by the scribes and Pharisees. Matthew adds to six of the woes the word *hypocrites,* almost like another title by which these teachers can be called. Jesus condemns making proselytes who will violate the law (verse 15); the swearing of hypocritical oaths (verses 16-17); tithing trivial things while neglecting justice, mercy, and faith (verses 23-24); outward observance of the law masking inward corruption (verses 25-28); honoring the dead prophets but wearing the mantle of those who killed the prophets (verses 29-33).

These verses come from a later time when Christians looked back to the crucifixion of Jesus. Now they see the leaders of Israel, fifty years later, repeating the same persecution against the followers of the Christ. When Jesus calls down on the Pharisees *all the righteous blood*, he utters the ultimate damnation against unfaithful servants.

Jesus Weeps Over Jerusalem (23:37-39)

We can read this lament in two ways: both as Jesus' vision of what was to happen (Jesus as prophet), and as lamentation of the Christian church for what had happened. We hear also an echo of the faith that the Christ would come again in the name of the Lord.

§ § § § § § §

The Message of Matthew 21–23

Surprisingly, in three chapters of the Gospel exclusively devoted to conflict with Pharisees, who no longer even exist in our world, we find much that speaks across the centuries to our time and our situation. The party of the Pharisees is long dead. Pharisaism is alive and well. The plumage by which we identify today's "Pharisees" is hypocrisy—the assuming of a false appearance of virtue or goodness.

Item (21:28-32): It is not uncommon for people to say Yes—sign up for some purpose, name in the newspaper, a show of participation. But when the cameras are turned off, many times these same people become no-shows.

Item (23:5-7): There is a pretense of conspicuous piety, but when the echoes of empty phrases have died away, nothing is seen or heard.

Item (23:25-26): Keeping up outward appearances can cover extortion and rapacity.

Item (23:27-28): Some persons give lip service to the "role models of old" but perpetuate the sins that cost them their lives.

Whether or not Jesus ever blasted a fig tree in quite the way the Gospel reports it, the story nevertheless carries an important message. The purpose of every tree is to bear fruit in its season. The tree that bears no fruit is best cut down. Likewise with faith, or with the church. If it does not bear the fruits of mercy, justice, goodness, and peace, it is worthless.

The parable of the rejected invitation is a warning to everyone who makes light of God's invitation to feast on divine grace and goodness. Lots of things seem more exciting. Do we really need grace all that much? Maybe some other time. Perhaps when we retire. But the commercials offer such wonderful things to make life full. The wheel of fortune spins, and we only go around once. So, we make light of it. So what?

Lots of people have nightmares of showing up at a wedding (or some other festival) wearing the wrong clothes. But this may be a "good" nightmare to have if we expect to show up in their number when the saints go marching in. The proper attire for any person who would be at God's reception is garments of praise, justice, peace, and humility, not in some outfit of our own concoction!

How much shall I render to Caesar today, and what do I owe God? No day dawns but that we have to face and answer that question. And we can't always say, This is for Caesar and that is for God. For more often than not, we render obedience to God through service to institutions and agencies of the civil state. And almost always the best way to serve the state is by fidelity to God.

§ § § § § § §

Matthew 24–25

Introduction to These Chapters

These two chapters form the fifth and final teaching discourse in the Gospel. Before working through the many blocks of material that Matthew has gathered here, one should be aware that chapter 24 is an *apocalypse,* a very different kind of literature from anything else in the Gospel. An apocalypse is a writing that purports to disclose or reveal a hidden meaning of events taking place in the world. Such writing almost always points to signs of the end time, whether the end of the world or the culmination of Israel's history. Chapter 24, which is mainly based on the Little Apocalypse of Mark 13, is filled with signs of the End. The principal sign of the End will be the *sign of the Son of man in heaven.* Then, says the apocalypse, *they will see the Son of man coming on the clouds of heaven (the sky)* (24:30).

The challenging problem for students of the Gospel presented by the Little Apocalypse is to know how much of it may be the authentic words of Jesus and how much may be the apocalyptic faith of Matthew or others writing after the destruction of Jerusalem in A.D. 70. Whether Jesus thought of himself as the Son of man is uncertain. Without question, first-century Christians believed Jesus the Christ would return *with power and great glory.* We shall address these problems in what follows. Here it may be sufficient to say that while the symbolic language of the apocalypse may not be literally true, it has a meaning that is eternally true.

Chapter 25 includes three extended parables on the Kingdom and the final judgment.

Here is an outline of chapters 24–25.

Destruction of the Temple (24:1-2)

Jews everywhere took understandable pride in the magnificent Jerusalem Temple being rebuilt by Herod in the time of Jesus. Even the disciples were caught up in unrestrained boasting. Jesus had sharper vision; he could see trouble ahead for the Temple and for the nation itself. Overwrought nationalism in Israel was on a collision course with Rome. The storm broke in full fury in A.D. 64 and the Temple was torn to pieces six years later. Jesus' response to the disciples' pride was as much a warning about their exultation in the stones of the Temple as it was a prediction of destruction.

False Teachers (24:3-8)

False teachers were a danger of which Jesus was aware. Even more did they pose a threat to the young churches in Matthew's time. Following the devastating defeat by the Romans in the Jewish War (A.D. 65–70), apocalyptic hope intensified as it replaced the fierce nationalism of Jesus' day. Matthew knew how vulnerable hopeful Christians were to the "I am the Christ" declarations of all kinds of prophets. The Gospel seeks to counter the belief of Christians that the End is just around the corner. *All these are the beginning of birth pains* (NIV, verse 8).

A Time of Tribulation (24:9-14)

These verses give us a picture of what was already happening. The first savage persecution of Christians broke out under the emperor Nero in A.D. 64. Even after Nero died in 68, Christians were beaten and lynched by raging mobs who believed fantastic rumors about the followers of Jesus. We read an example of this in the story of the riot in Ephesus (Acts 19:21-41). In the heat of this torment many Christians "fell away" (see Revelation 24); their love grew cold.

Earlier Jesus had declared his mission to be *to the lost sheep of Israel* (10:6). Now he announces that the End cannot be until the gospel has been preached throughout the *whole world* (see also 28:20). Such a widening of purpose was the consequence of the rejection of Jesus by the leaders of Israel.

The Gospel promises that all who remain faithful through persecution will be saved (24:13). Christians needed such strong assurance as they faced overpowering tribulation.

Signs of the End (24:15-28)

The desolating sacrilege (NRSV; NIV = *abomination that causes desolation*) recalls Daniel 11:31. In that instance Daniel has in mind the statue of Zeus by which the king of Syria profaned the Temple in 168 B.C. This happened at the time of the Maccabees, leaders of Judea in the struggle against Hellenistic culture. The Little

Apocalypse (Mark 13; Luke 21; Matthew 24) predicts a comparable Roman sacrilege in the Temple. Such an abomination had already occurred when Matthew's Gospel appeared. The horrors that Jesus foresaw are amply confirmed by the Jewish historian Josephus in his eyewitness account in the *Wars of the Jews.* Josephus records that more than one million persons died in this first-century holocaust. The ones from whom this apocalypse was handed down believed the anguish and human devastation was so great that the Lord shortened the time until the End (24:22).

Let the reader understand (verse 15) is a signal of a hidden meaning, which Christians would perceive.

The coming of the Son of man will be like lightning, not hidden but visible for everyone to see (verse 27).

Signs of the Son of Man (24:29-31)

The appearance of heavenly phenomena is characteristic of apocalyptic revelation (see Isaiah 13:10). Such signs confirm in the minds of the faithful that God controls the creation. The faithful do not await these events with any fear, for the *angels . . . will gather his elect* (24:31). When Matthew recalls the visions of Daniel, the image of the Son of man flashes with unprecedented brightness, because Christians believed that the Messiah had already appeared in Jesus; now they awaited his return. Surely Matthew perceived this sign to be the fulfillment of Daniel 7:13-14.

Some scholars believe that the phrase *coming on the clouds of heaven* describes the Son of man's coming *to* God in the Resurrection, an interpretation strengthened by three passages in John's Gospel (John 3:14; 8:28; 12:32). However that may be, the early Christians anticipated the *return* of the Son of man.

Lessons of the Fig Tree (24:32-35)

The apocalypse does here what Jesus again and again warned his disciples not to do: It looks for signs of the

End. *When you see all these things, you know that it (he) . . . is near* (verse 33). The stress on signs we can more likely read as the later words of the apocalypse. The words on watchfulness that follow immediately we have every reason to attribute to Jesus.

The Need for Watchfulness (24:36-44)

Watch! Upon this world Jesus puts exceeding stress. Like the thief that comes in the night, people can be caught entirely unprepared. Jesus warns that the Son of man will come at an hour we do not expect. The admonition to *watch* prepares the way for the three parables of the coming of the Kingdom that follow: the master and his servants, the wise and foolish maidens, and the talents.

The Householder and the Servants (24:45-51)

When Jesus originally told this parable, it may have represented a warning about responsibility and stewardship. People are expected to discharge faithfully the duties entrusted to them. For example, Israel is to be faithful to all that the covenant requires. In this apocalyptic setting of Matthew's Gospel, the urgency of the parable is intensified. The injunction to faithful obedience is unmistakably directed to the leaders (deacons) of the young churches. They are expecting the master to return, but they do not know when. As found in verse 48, *He has been delayed* (NRSV) or *he is staying away a long time* (NIV). This may reflect the puzzlement of Christians as to why the Christ has not returned as they anticipated. In the meantime they must not grow lax in carrying out the responsibilities of caring for the young churches, their leaders, and the "little ones."

Wise and Foolish Maidens (25:1-12)

Like the preceding parable of the householder and his servants, the story of the wise and foolish maidens has had more than one application. The parable belongs in the long tradition of Israel, the bride of Yahweh (Isaiah 54:6; Hosea 2:16). In the first place, Jesus clearly points to the failure of Israel's leaders to be watchful custodians and keepers of the covenant. Jesus must also have intended to warn the leaders of the new Israel, what was to become the Christian church, against irresponsibility and sleep. The story is a parable, not an allegory; we do not invest all the details with symbolic meaning. It has one message: readiness! The foolish maidens seem to have relied on the good will of the bridegroom to dismiss their irresponsibility and unreadiness.

The Talents (25:13-30)

This parable has been used in an irresponsible way on account of the word *talent*. In Jesus' story *talent* does not mean natural capabilities, for example in music or athletic ability. *Talent* was originally a measure of weight; by Jesus' time it had become a monetary unit, a very expensive one, figured at around $1,000, quite a fortune in that day. The point of the parable is that two of the servants used the opportunity or responsibility given to them in a productive way. The third servant did not; he gave back only what had been given to him. Like the parable of the householder (24:45-51), this story makes plain the truth that God expects Israel, and subsequently the Christian church, to produce the fruits of righteousness and faith with what has been entrusted to them. Luke concludes the parable in his Gospel (Luke 12:48): *From everyone who has been given much, much will be demanded; and from the one who has been entrusted with much, much more will be asked* (NIV).

The master's attitude and the punishment he meted out to the slothful servant may seem harsh. But the severity of the punishment is the measure by which people are to realize their obligation to turn the gifts of the covenant into good works and deeds of love and mercy.

The Judgment (25:31-46)

The three parables of the apocalypse all end on a note of judgment. Accounts are to be rendered; in the case of the wide and foolish maidens, some entered the house, while others were excluded. Now we come to the parable that stands at the epitome of the Gospel teaching about judgment.

Because Matthew chose this parable as the culmination of Jesus' teaching ministry, and placed it immediately before the beginning of the Passion narrative, we infer that it has unparalleled significance for Jesus and in the understanding of the early church. The parable reveals several things of central importance to the Gospel.

Nowhere are the priorities and commitments of Jesus' life and ministry shown with greater clarity than in the imagery of this parable. The compassion pictured here is expected of every follower of Jesus.

The people will be judged at the end time by how they responded to the needs of the least of those whom Jesus embraced as brothers and sisters. So the lives we now live become in fact our judgment at the End.

The parable is ambiguous about Jesus and the Son of man. He does not say, "I am the Son of man." But the one whom he announces as the heavenly figure coming in glory the Christians following the Resurrection readily identified with Jesus the Christ.

The righteous did these things not because they expected to be rewarded, but out of compassion. They did not know that the Son of man (or Jesus) was manifest in the hungry, the thirsty, the prisoner, or the stranger.

§ § § § § § §

The Message of Matthew 24–25

These chapters have been grossly misused by Christians across the centuries. People have made it a hunting ground for texts supposedly forecasting apocalyptic events in every age since the Resurrection. We abuse the Scriptures when we make them a horoscope of predictions. Chapters 24 and 25 are rather a warning and an invitation. The Gospel warns us about the consequences of infidelity or indifference, and invites us to choose faithfulness and compassion, and to enter into opportunities and responsibilities of the community of faith.

One word catches the essential meaning of these two chapters (at least up to the parable of the Last Judgment): *Watch!* No one knows, *not even the Son,* when the end time may come. For each of us there comes an end time beyond which lie no tomorrows in this life. Ahead for our nation lies some judgment of history. And for the world, a cataclysm will come from which none may hide. But Jesus bids us watch. And the Gospel tells us how to wait and be ready.

Lord, open to us. The cry of the maidens shut out of the marriage feast haunts us, because it reminds us that no one improvises a faith in the moment of crisis when it is needed. No one suddenly fills a life with compassion and Christian witness when the account must be rendered.

The parable of the Last Judgment shows us the imperative of love's expectation. It tells how we are to live in response to the love that we know God has for us.

§ § § § § § §

Matthew 26

Introduction to This Chapter

Chapters 26 and 27 constitute what has come to be
known as the Passion story, the narrative account of
Jesus' final days in Jerusalem before his death on the
cross. Chapter 26 is the longest chapter in the Gospel; 26
and 27 taken together contain 141 verses, thirteen per
cent of the whole book. But more important than
comparative length is the content of these pages: the
conspiracy against Jesus by the high priests and elders;
his Last Supper with his disciples; his agony and arrest in
Gethsemane; the two trials before Caiaphas and Pilate,
which condemned him to death; his torture by the
Romans; the Crucifixion on Calvary, and his burial in the
tomb. These are the definitive events in the Christian
story in which believers ever since have found the
primary meaning of their faith.

All evidence indicates that the Passion story was the
earliest part of the Gospel to be brought together,
circulating first in oral form and then as a written
document. Mark 14–15 is as close as we can get to that
original source, long since disappeared as a separate
document. Matthew had no other independent Passion
material beyond those chapters in Mark. Matthew
introduces a number of Old Testament verses that he
believes were being fulfilled by the events in the story.

Chapter 26 begins with Jesus' fourth announcement of

the Crucifixion and carries the story through the hearing before Caiaphas and Peter's denial.

Here is an outline of chapter 26.

Jesus' Announcement (26:1-2)

The chapter opens with the familiar transition sentence with which Matthew closes each of the five teaching sections in the Gospel. Immediately Jesus announces to his disciples (for the fourth time, following 16:21; 17:22; 20:18) that he is going to his death at the hands of the chief priests and the elders of the people. The verse sounds as the theme whose enactment will be the summit of the Gospel.

Conspiracy of Priests and Elders (26:3-5)

Caiaphas was high priest from A.D. 18–36, a comparatively long tenure. He held his office at the favor of the Roman authorities. If the chief priests and elders participated in this decision the whole affair originated as a Sanhedrin plot. It was legal perhaps, but it was cloaked with secrecy and shrouded in dubious morality.

The Sanhedrin was the supreme Jewish council, having legislative, executive, and judicial functions related to whatever was of no consequence to Rome. The high priest presided over this ruling body. The conspirators decided to act speedily and in secret, hoping to have Jesus the troublemaker out of the way before Passover began. They feared a popular uprising of pilgrims from Galilee in support of Jesus.

The Anointing at Bethany (26:6-13)

Bethany is a small village about a mile and a half east of Jerusalem. In this village lived Mary, Martha, and Lazarus, whom Jesus raised from the dead (John 11:1-44). We assume that Simon, in whose house this incident took place, was a leper who had been healed. (Compare Matthew's story with a similar occasion reported in Luke 7:36-38.) The Gospel does not tell us in whose house Jesus may have stayed during these final nights of his life.

The early Christians would readily tell this beautiful story about Jesus. They would want to remember his gracious response to the nameless woman's act. But Matthew has another purpose for placing the incident here: to contrast the devoted awareness of the woman with the insensitivity of the disciples. Jesus knew that he was to die within days; the disciples should have known. Yet it was the woman who anointed him in a symbolic way for his burial. In no way should Jesus' words to his disciples be taken as indifference to the poor. The poor they are to care for always. The disciples seem oblivious to what looms ahead of them, slow-witted once again.

Judas's Betrayal to the Chief Priests (26:14-16)

What Judas betrayed to the priests has never been understood for certain, nor why he did it. People have surmised that Judas took the priests where they could find Jesus at night, away from the crowds. Others have subjected that Judas told the authorities what Jesus had said about himself as Messiah (Son of man), if indeed Jesus ever explicitly identified himself as such. If Judas revealed the so-called "messianic secret" to the priests, they could charge Jesus with blasphemy, which, of course, they did.

Even more puzzling is *why* Judas should do this. Was

it greed? Was it jealousy (Judas was the only Judean among a band of Galileans)? Some have supposed Judas was disillusioned. Events were getting out of hand as hopes for a triumph over the powers of Jerusalem and Rome grew dim. A notion widely held imagines that Judas thought he could force Jesus' hand by turning him over to the priests, where he would be compelled to do something to inaugurate the new age. Some have even thought that Jesus conspired with Judas to turn him in to the authorities, hastening the Crucifixion by which God's purposes would be more swiftly accomplished. Nothing in these verses answers any of these questions for us.

Thirty shekels of silver is the price paid to a *worthless* (*foolish*) *shepherd* in Zechariah's vision (Zechariah 11:12, 15). It was the price of a slave; the early Christians would have sensed the irony of the Christ who gave his life as a ransom for the whole world, sold as a slave for a paltry thirty pieces of silver. The whole of Zechariah 11 foreshadows the event of the Crucifixion.

We notice also the repeated use of the verb *hand over*. It was used in verse 2 and even in verse 15 in the NIV, and is repeated in 27:2, 18, 26, emphasizing that Jesus was handed over from one authority or group to another. Everyone who had a part in the affair shared the guilt. Jesus had relinquished his power to resist or alter the course of events. (See John 19:11 where Jesus tells Pilate that he would have no power over him had it not been given to him from above.)

The Last Supper (26:17-29)

Nothing in all the Gospels is more familiar and important to Christians than the Last Supper. From the very beginning it became a model for the eucharist (Communion, the Lord's Supper). No Sunday has ever dawned since the church began to hold eucharists that the Last Supper has not been memorialized.

In this commentary we cannot even raise, let alone

untangle, all of the persistent questions with regard to the Last Supper. These questions gather around the issues of the day on which the supper was held and how the supper is related to the Passover. We can suggest tentative answers to the questions, knowing that whatever the answers to these questions, the faith of the church, which is rooted in the Lord's Supper, remains unchanged.

The first day of the feast of Unleavened Bread was the day when preparations were made for the Passover, the holiest day in the Jewish calendar. If John's Gospel gives us the more accurate chronology for Holy Week, Jesus was crucified Friday afternoon on Passover Eve, when the Passover lambs were being sacrificed. The Last Supper then was held the night before (or, in the judgment of many scholars, two or even three nights before, with the possibility that the trials of Jesus may have taken longer than the time reported in the Synoptic Gospels). Christians from the beginning have recognized the symbolism of Jesus being sacrificed at the time of Passover (see 1 Corinthians 5:7: *Christ, our paschal (Passover) lamb, has been sacrificed*). The meal may not have been a true Passover; no mention is made of lamb or bitter herbs being eaten, food that was always served at Passover. In any case the early church immediately recognized the symbolism of Jesus' death and Passover.

These verses indicate that careful preparation had been made for this meal that was to become so significant for the church. A room was made ready (see also Mark 14:15). The disciples served, as the deacons were to do in the churches.

The earliest account of what happened at the meal we find in 1 Corinthians 11:23-26. That letter can be dated around A.D. 50, just twenty years after the event itself. Paul's report differs only slightly from the account in Mark, which Matthew copied. Very early the church had formulated the tradition going back to the Last Supper.

The symbolic words *took . . . blessed (gave thanks) . . . broke . . . gave* were spoken as part of the meal itself, not as a separate ceremony. Jesus invests the elements of bread and cup with the meaning of his death by which the forgiven faithful would enter a new covenant (26:28). The words of the Last Supper bring to mind the words spoken by Jesus at the feeding of the two multitudes on the mountainsides where Jesus *took, blessed, broke,* and *gave* (14:19; 15:36). See "The Message of Matthew 26" below for further reflection.

Peter's Promise (26:30-35)

Matthew reports this forecast as fulfillment of Zechariah 13:7. Jesus here anticipates his appearance in Galilee following the Resurrection (28:16). Jesus knew Peter better than Peter knew himself.

The Garden of Gethsemane (26:36-46)

Here is where Jesus wins his victory over Satan. Alone, with the disciples sleeping (a metaphor for infidelity), Jesus chooses not to run away, as it would be tempting and easy to do. Instead he stays to bear witness through his death to God's forgiving love. No one hears Jesus' prayers; the disciples must have known by intuition in retrospect how he would have prayed. Notice that Jesus takes with him Peter, James, and John, the same three who went with him up the mount of Transfiguration (17:1).

Jesus' Arrest (26:47-56)

The crowd that came from the high priests must have expected forceful resistance; they came heavily armed with swords and clubs. To identify Jesus with a kiss may have been an insult. Disciples were not accustomed to greet their teacher on their own initiative; that would have implied equality. That might not have been the case between Jesus and his disciples, but it was a rule generally honored among the Jews. Jesus' rebuke of the disciple who struck the servant of the high priest with his sword is pointed at all who imagine that God's kingdom can ever either conquer or be defended by the sword.

Hearing Before the Sanhedrin (26:57-68)

Was the Sanhedrin assembled illegally at night to carry out the predetermined plan to execute Jesus? Or was this an informal hearing to get evidence, which could later be used in a formal indictment? And why were they apparently willing to violate their own law that a capital punishment could not be executed until a whole day had passed between sentencing and execution? These questions remain unanswered. But they are moot questions in view of how the whole affair ended before Pilate.

The Sanhedrin needed a charge by which to condemn Jesus. It is not clear whether, at the time of this trial, in certain cases of blasphemy the Jews had the power of capital punishment. It may have been so because it was on the charge of blasphemy that they first sought indictment. Witnesses could not agree on any charge until two were brought forward with the charge that Jesus said he could destroy and rebuild the Temple in three days. It was a fantastic claim, but it was not a capital offense. Caiaphas then asked Jesus outright if he were the Christ. Jesus does not deny the claim. Now the Sanhedrin has a charge under which Jesus can be delivered to the Roman governor, Pontius Pilate. In the thought of both Israel and Rome *messiah* was a political title and authority. Rome might not care about *Son of man*, an unfamiliar religious figure. But a political ruler of Israel—that they understood and found intolerable! Caiaphas knew that Jesus posed no political or military threat to Rome. But Pilate did not know that. We will see in the next chapter how Caiaphas blackmailed Pilate into carrying out the death plot of the Sanhedrin.

It is true that in the mind of Caiaphas Jesus was a

blaspheming heretic. *Coming on the clouds of heaven* was presumptuous arrogance for anyone to claim for himself. Had they not been afraid of losing their power, they might have regarded that claim as nonsense. But in addition, the Sadducees did not believe in the resurrection; Jesus implied that he would be raised and that angels would accompany him at his coming. At least that is what Caiaphas heard Jesus say. These were matters internal to Jewish religious belief, of little concern to Rome. Where Caiaphas was most culpable was in sending Jesus to Pilate under charges the high priest knew were fraudulent. Understandably the Sanhedrin preferred to make Pilate the executioner who would dispose of Jesus. Let the blood be on Rome's head and hands.

Peter's Denial (26:69-75)

Three times in Gethsemane Jesus prayed, *"Remove this cup from me; yet, not what I want, but what you want"* (NRSV). And *three times* Peter slept while Jesus prayed. Now *three times* Peter denies he even knew Jesus. We must not miss the irony of Peter's denial, using the same words the bridegroom speaks to the foolish maidens in the parable, *I do not know you* (25:12).

§ § § § § § §

The Message of Matthew 26

The Lord's Supper is a time to remember the meal Jesus ate with his disciples on the night when he was betrayed. Each time we drink the cup at Communion we receive forgiveness of sins. And we remember Jesus' promise that he will drink the cup anew with us in God's kingdom. That promise and that gift make Communion an occasion no less for joy than for sorrow.

Peter sometimes stands as a mirror in which we see ourselves reflected. "I will never fall away," he fervently proclaims. But in the same night, maybe no more than six hours later, he cries with equal ardor, "I do not know the man." On the mount of Transfiguration Peter wants to build three booths so the disciples and Jesus can stay there, little understanding why Jesus must go down the mountain to his death (17:4). And while Peter sleeps his master goes far into the valley of the shadow of death, alone! Words echo from the apostle Paul: *So if you think you are standing firm, be careful that you don't fall!* (1 Corinthians 10:12).

One of the most pathetic sentences in the entire Gospel occurs in 26:56: *All the disciples deserted him and fled* (26:56). We have read much in this Gospel about the responsibility of true shepherds of the sheep. Here is a frightening picture of sheep abandoning the shepherd! Shepherds need warning about fidelity to shepherding. And who cannot think of shepherds who forsook the sheep? But sheep can also forsake the shepherd and run away. Or, as a preacher once reminded his flock, "Sheep can nibble themselves lost."

§ § § § § § §

Matthew 27

Introduction to This Chapter

As we look over the whole Passion story, chapters
26–27, we see that it can be divided into three main
events, as an aid in remembering: (1) Jesus and the
disciples, their preparation for the Passion, 26:6-46;
(2) Jesus' hearing before Caiaphas and his condemnation
by the Sanhedrin, 26:47-75; (3) Jesus' trial, condemnation,
and crucifixion by the Romans, 27:1-66.

A succession of ten episodes comprises chapter 27.
These have to do with the trial before Pilate, and Jesus'
torture and death at the hands of the Romans. The
account of Judas's suicide is a powerful reminder of the
trail that led to this awful moment. The unexpected
appearance of the women on Calvary and at the
tomb—none of the disciples were any longer to be
seen—is the glimmer of things to come on *the first day of
the week.*

Here is an outline of chapter 27.

   I. The Chief Priests Deliver Jesus (27:1-2)
  II. The Suicide of Judas Iscariot (27:3-10)
 III. Jesus Before Pilate (27:11-23)
  IV. Jesus Condemned to Death (27:24-26)
   V. Jesus Is Mocked and Scourged (27:27-31)
  VI. Jesus' Crucifixion and Death (27:32-50)
 VII. Signs at the Crucifixion (27:51-54)
VIII. The Women at Calvary (27:55-56)
  IX. The Entombment (27:57-61)
   X. A Guard Placed at the Tomb (27:62-66)

The Chief Priests Deliver Jesus (27:1-2)

The action of the Sanhedrin in turning Jesus over to the Romans leaves unanswered the question as to whether they could themselves have put him to death. The evidence seems to indicate that capital punishment could be carried out only by Rome. In any case, considering Jesus' popularity among the people, it was better for the priests and elders not to have the onus of Jesus' death on their heads. Apparently this early morning meeting of the Sanhedrin was called simply to ratify what they had plotted during the night.

The Suicide of Judas Iscariot (27:3-10)

This scene of Judas's attempt to undo his betrayal of Jesus is pathetic and revealing. Admitting now that he has betrayed *innocent blood*, he desperately tries, by returning the money, to have Jesus released. As though thirty pieces of silver would have any effect on the decision of the rulers to put Jesus to death! It would seem that Judas neither expects nor wants to see Jesus dead, but wishes to call forth his decisive showdown with all the authorities. Seeing that such will not happen, and that he cannot erase a single line of the betrayal, he goes out in a craze of remorse to kill himself.

The scene also suggests that the chief priests knew the thirty pieces of silver were blood money—payment for the death of an innocent man. Even they had scruples about putting that money into the Temple treasury. An appropriate use for the blood money was to purchase a burial ground for strangers who died in Jerusalem. Acts 1:18-19 pictures a different, though no less violent, end for Judas. Apparently he could not trust that God would forgive him.

Jesus Before Pilate (27:11-23)

Pontius Pilate was governor or procurator of Judea from A.D. 26–36, an office held by appointment of

Emperor Tiberius. His principal responsibility was to keep order in the province and enforce obedience to Roman rule and regulation. Pilate's palace was on the Mediterranean coast at Caesarea; at times, when the city was thronged with people and trouble seemed likely to flare up, he moved up to Jerusalem.

The Sanhedrin has sent Jesus to Pilate on the charges of treason and subversion. They know these charges are false. Even Pilate senses that the whole affair has been trumped up. But he is the keeper of law and order; the quickest way to fall into disfavor with the emperor is to let a riot get out of hand. An angry Sanhedrin, perhaps even making trouble with Caesar, Pilate would not risk. In Luke 23:2 we can read the charge on which the chief priests delivered Jesus to the Roman governor. To Pilate's question, "Are you the king of the Jews?" Matthew reports that Jesus gave no direct answer. Quite probably Jesus could not admit to being a king in any sense that Pilate would understand.

Matthew obviously tries to present Pilate in a more favorable light than other evidence suggests. Pilate disregarded the religious sensitivities of the Jews, despoiled their Temple treasury for his own ends, and marked his rule in Judea with brutality. But Matthew's purpose is to put the primary guilt for Jesus' death on the chief priests.

Some manuscripts give the name of the notorious prisoner as *Jesus Barabbas. Barabbas* means literally *son of the father*. The choice that Pilate gives to the people, all unwittingly, is thus between "son of the father" and "Son of the Father." If it is true that Barabbas was an insurrectionist, Pilate may have hoped the people would welcome being relieved of such a revolutionary "freedom fighter." Thus he would be able to dismiss Jesus as innocent. The chief priests accepted no such trade-off; Jesus threatened their position infinitely more than Barabbas.

This is the only Gospel in which Pilate's wife recounts her dream that Jesus is innocent. Matthew would understand the dream as a warning from God.

We should note, in passing, the account found only in Luke 23:6-12 of Pilate sending Jesus to Herod. It seems unlikely that Pilate would allow Herod any authority in such a capital affair. The story may have been an accommodation to the report in Acts 4:25-28 that Herod and Pontius Pilate carried out the plan that had been "predestined" to take place.

Jesus Condemned to Death (27:24-26)

It has become a part of our language to say that we "wash our hands of the matter." The image goes back to Pilate. The cry of the crowd, *His blood be on us*, is Matthew's way of establishing the guilt emphatically on the Jews. (For additional information see below, "The Message of Matthew 27.")

Jesus Is Mocked and Scourged (27:27-31)

It was the custom to make brutal sport with the condemned before their execution. The symbols with which the soldiers regaled Jesus are those of royalty. Perhaps the ultimate irony lies in these verses. Jesus was innocent of the charges brought against him. But he was truly a king, and they did not know it.

Jesus' Crucifixion and Death (27:32-50)

Crucifixion must be one of the cruelist, most agonizing deaths ever conceived. The condemned man was made to carry the heavy crossbar of the instrument of his death, the upright remaining in place on the hill of death. The brutality inflicted during the torture would drain much of the strength and blood of the condemned man. It left Jesus too weak to make it all the way to the top of Golgotha. The hill was so named not only because it was the place where crucifixions were carried out, but also because it is thought to have been in the shape of a human skull.

Simon of *Cyrene* (a place on the north coast of Africa) was probably a Jew living in that distant land who had come as a pilgrim to the Passover in the Holy City. Mark 15:21 names the two sons of Simon, strongly suggesting that the family became Christians some time after Jesus' death and resurrection.

When a person is crucified, either his arms are tied or his hands are nailed to the ends of the cross beam. His feet are then lashed or nailed to the foot of the upright, slightly above the ground, and his body supported underneath to prolong the agony. Death comes either by strangulation, loss of blood, dehydration, or a ruptured heart. It sometimes took days for a person to die; Jesus' time on the cross was mercifully short—three hours.

Dying victims were offered an opiate to make them unconscious in the final paroxysm. Jesus refused it.

One should read all four Gospel accounts (Mark 15; Luke 23; John 18:28-19:42). Mark and Matthew report only one "word" spoken from the cross, the word of dereliction. These are the first words of Psalm 22. Jesus may have remembered the triumphant ending of that psalm. But we cannot doubt the sense of utter abandonment expressed in that cry. John and Luke, drawing upon independent traditions, record additional words, which were to become precious in the memory of the church.

The Romans not only humiliated Jesus, but insulted the Jews as well. By the title they placed above Jesus' head they blatantly shamed the Jewish people by calling this disgraced victim their *king*. The chief priests joined in deriding Jesus through his last hours with the mocking taunts that he could not save himself.

The chief priests seemed to have achieved their purpose: to kill Jesus and to expose to ridicule all of his claims (27:42-43).

Signs at the Crucifixion (27:51-54)

The rent veil of the Temple, the earthquake, the tombs being opened, and the confession of the centurion are all symbolic manifestations of the meaning of the death of Jesus. (See "The Message of Matthew 27.")

The Women at Calvary (27:55-56)

Peter weeping bitterly (26:75) and Judas hanging himself (27:5) are the last we see of any of the disciples until after the Resurrection. It has been suggested that while their disappearance may have been due to cowardice, nevertheless the Lord needed them even more in the days beyond the Resurrection. It may be providential that these followers of Jesus became invisible while the heat of the Crucifixion was on. In the mysterious irony of the cross they abandoned Jesus at Calvary, only to become his apostles in later days.

The women did not forsake Jesus. Among them were the two Marys and the mother of James and John. Only the Fourth Gospel places Mary, the mother of Jesus, at the Crucifixion.

The Entombment (27:57-61)

Arimathea may have been a town somewhat north and west of Jerusalem, on the lower slopes of the hill country. Mark tells us that Joseph was a member of the council, perhaps the Jerusalem Sanhedrin, more probably in the town of his birth. He was either rich, or highly respected, or both. Apparently he had acquired a tomb for himself in Jerusalem. Into this sepulchre he placed the body of Jesus. This was a gracious act, because the tomb would never be used again after an executed criminal had been placed therein. The Gospel does not mention Joseph before this episode, nor does it tell us how he got to be a disciple. He was simply available with a resource when it was needed. The body had to be removed from the cross before it polluted the sabbath at sundown. The women had not enough time even to prepare Jesus' body for proper burial. They would come to do this as soon as the sabbath had passed.

A Guard Placed at the Tomb (27:62-66)

This detail may not be historical, the story being added later when rumors began to circulate that the disciples had stolen the body and then spread the report of the Resurrection. The purpose of the story was to say to later Christians that in no way could Pilate "secure" the tomb against God's power to raise Jesus from the dead.

§ § § § § § §

The Message of Matthew 27

We find the deepest meaning of the cross not in the physical details of the Passion, but beneath, above, within, and beyond Jesus' death on Calvary. It is important to know the literal facts of what happened at Golgotha. But for the meaning of what happened we turn back to Isaiah 53:4-5, 12: *And by his wounds (bruises) we are healed.* We turn forward to Romans 5:8: *While we were still sinners Christ died for us.* We turn upward in our imagination to John 12:31-33. *I, when I am lifted up from the earth, will draw all people to myself* (NRSV). We look inward in faith as did "the two of them" at Emmaus, Luke 24:31: *Their eyes were opened and they recognized him.*

The blood of Jesus' death cannot be washed from the hands of Pilate. We can still hear the splash of water in that bowl. The Roman governor's futile gesture comes as a reminder that none can wash their hands of crucifixions, then or now. Forgiveness, possibly. Accountability, certainly!

For nearly two thousand years the Gospel of Matthew has regrettably been the fountainhead of appalling anti-Semitism. From this verse people have tried to build a case against the whole Jewish people: *They crucified the Lord* (verse 25). In the same spirit one could say: "The French burned Joan of Arc at the stake." "The English burned Thomas Cranmer." "The Americans hung the witches at Salem." Jesus was crucified at the instigation of certain high priests who feared for their power. But to attribute such a miscarriage of justice and morality to a whole nation is unconscionable. We grossly misread the Gospel of Matthew when we transfer its religious antipathies to the twentieth century.

The symbolic "signs," visible only to the eyes of faith, continue to show what the Crucifixion means. The veil of

Temple religion, designed to keep God *in* the sanctuary and people *out*, was rent from top to bottom. The whole earth has been shaken by what God did on that hilltop. People no longer need to fear an eternity locked in tombs; the cross/Resurrection has split open our confinement in death. And people of every race and nation still declare: "Truly this is the Son of God."

Against what adversaries did Jesus have to contend in the Passion! He dealt with the envy of the high priests, the timidity of the disciples, and the betrayal of those he trusted. He also encountered Pilate's fears, the soldiers' cruelty, the mocking derision of the people, the insecurity of a Roman governor who tried to "stonewall" the Resurrection. But thanks be to God who gives us the victory (over all these things) through our Lord Jesus Christ.

§ § § § § § §

Matthew 28

Introduction to This Chapter

Chapter 28, with its report of the Resurrection, stands not only as the climax in the story of Jesus; it also serves as the keystone in the arch of Matthew's Gospel. All of Matthew's purpose is fulfilled in the short narrative of Resurrection/Commission.

The Gospel opens with the announcement that Jesus shall be called *Emmanuel, God with us* (1:23). The very last words of the last chapter reaffirm that proclamation: *"I am with you always, to the end of the age"* (verse 20). But with us now is the power of the risen Lord.

The beginnings of the mission in the name of Christ appear throughout the Gospel (10:5-8; 22:9-10). That mission is now ratified in the commissioning of the disciples for their mission to the whole world by their risen Lord: *Go and make disciples of all nations* (verse 19).

It is here reported that the disciples *worshiped him* (verse 17). The Greek verb Matthew uses for *worship* is the same verb John uses to report Jesus' words, *the true worshipers will worship the Father in spirit and in truth* (John 4:23). The inference is clear that the young Christian church is to bow before its risen Lord even as the faithful have always worshiped Yahweh. Christian worship now takes on a new dimension toward the risen Lord.

Everything that I have commanded you (verse 20), the entire teaching of the five discourses or books of Matthew's Gospel, is now authenticated. This is what the church is to hear, to believe, and to teach to all nations.

137

One might say that by the Resurrection God puts the stamp of divine approval on what Jesus has taught.

So we see all twenty-seven chapters of Matthew coming toward and flowing into this final chapter. This is the faith we hear spoken in the preaching of the Acts of the Apostles, in the letters of Paul, and in the testimony of the writer of the book of Revelation. Perhaps we wee in this chapter more than in any other part of the Gospel Matthew's prophetic purpose. His ruling interest here obviously goes beyond the historical account of what happened following the Crucifixion. It moves on to what the event of the Resurrection must mean to the Christian church, which has come into being.

Here is an outline of chapter 28.

   I. At the Tomb (28:1-10)
      A. Dawn, earthquake, and angel (28:1-4)
      B. "He is not here" (28:5-6)
      C. "Go and tell his disciples" (28:7-8)
      D. Jesus meets the women (28:9-10)
  II. The Guard Tries a Cover-up (28:11-15)
 III. The Great Commission (28:16-20)

Dawn, Earthquake, and Angel (28:1-4)

Of all the followers of Jesus, the two Marys alone saw the burial and knew where the tomb was. They now came on *the first day of the week,* probably to give Jesus' body the proper rite of burial (Mark 16:1), a ministration of great importance. Matthew omits the mention of this purpose. In his account the guard at the tomb would very likely have prevented any approach to the body. *Dawn* locates the event in time. It also has theological significance; this day was truly to be the *dawn* of the new age.

Only Matthew's Gospel reports an earthquake. In this regard Matthew draws upon a tradition as to how the stone was rolled away. In all probability the rock tomb was closed by a large round stone, which rolled in a trough to cover the opening into the rock face. Women could not have rolled it back to admit entrance. Mark reports the women wondering, *"Who will roll the stone away from the entrance of the tomb?"* (NIV) This is a detail omitted in the Gospel of Matthew. An earthquake would be seen as an act of divine intervention, along with the presence of an angel. These two manifestations reportedly stunned the guards into trauma and insensibility.

It should be understood that the tomb was opened, whether by the earthquake in Matthew's Gospel or by the power of God expressed in some unknown way in the other three Gospels, not in order to release Jesus from his grave, but to allow the Marys to look within.

"He Is Not Here" (28:5-6)

Matthew follows Mark in the words that the angel speaks: *He is not here.* Luke puts the announcement in the form of a question: *Why do you look for the living among the dead?* (Luke 24:5). In all four Gospels the women verify the empty tomb (Mark 16:6; Luke 24:3; John 20:12). That the women found the tomb empty is central to the various Resurrection narratives.

"Go and Tell His Disciples" (28:7-8)

Central also in the several traditions is the role the women carried out. *Go and tell his disciples.* They became the link between the living Jesus and the disciples in hiding, who presumably knew nothing about the earthshaking event taking place where Jesus had been buried. No doubt if God had willed it so, the risen Christ could have come to the disciples wherever they were. But that's not what happened first. *The women were the first evangelists of the Resurrection.* That glory will always be theirs.

Jesus Meets the Women (28:9-10)

This sparsely reported meeting with Jesus as the women leave the empty tomb has little of the dramatic impact of that first encounter as told by Luke and John. Apparently Matthew's purpose is to make doubly sure that the disciples get themselves back to Galilee. Both Luke and John include accounts of Resurrection appearances to the disciples in Jerusalem. It appears to have been important to Luke to identify the Christian mission as beginning in Jerusalem (Luke 24:47; Acts 1:8). Matthew emphasizes that Jesus appears to his disciples in Galilee as he had promised. (The meeting in Galilee certainly has further purpose; see below, 28:16).

The Guard Tries a Cover-up (28:11-15)

Here we have an interruption in the narrative. What difference does it make what the chief priests said or did? In the late years of the first century it made all the difference in the world. If the chief priests could spread the rumor and make it stick that the disciples stole the body and then broadcast the unbelievable tale that Jesus rose from the dead, they could thoroughly discredit the report of a resurrection. By knocking out the tale of Jesus being raised from the dead, the whole Christian gospel could be unmasked as fraud. In the atmosphere of enmity between Christian converts and the Jerusalem authorities in Matthew's time, it was crucial that Christians be told how the chief priests and sentries at the tomb conspired to try to disparage the reports of a resurrection.

The Great Commission (28:16-20)

We may not be far off the mark if we suppose that Matthew was mindful of Moses receiving a covenant for Israel on Mount Sinai. Now Jesus gives to the disciples a new commission and mandate from a mountain in Galilee, the scene of his most received teaching. The Gospel fails to tell us on what mountain the Great Commission was given and received. Was it the place from which the Sermon on the Mount had first been heard? Or was it the mount on which Peter, James, and

John saw Jesus transfigured? We can only wonder. But the principal point is that Jesus' ministry was given a divine sanction and authority.

With the Resurrection the authority conceded to Jesus in his earthly ministry has now been elevated to the authority of heaven. So his teachings become more than the mere words of the Great Teacher. They are now the divine imperative, confirmed by God's raising Jesus from the dead. The Resurrection fulfills Daniel 7:14.

They worshiped him. This statement is not just history. It also describes the church in Matthew's time. Indeed, the time had now come when people were to worship Jesus the Christ. *But some doubted.* Was the evangelist thinking here of Thomas, the doubter? That may well have been true, although Matthew contains no incident of Thomas's doubting. More likely he spoke of the congregation of his church. Not everyone believed with robust faith. Some may have doubted. Matthew reminds his readers that it was even so among the twelve disciples.

The Commission is to be a missionary: *Go and make disciples of all nations.* This imperative goes beyond where the disciples were sent on their first mission, *nowhere among the Gentiles* (NRSV, 10:5-6).

The Commission is to *baptize.* And the full trinitarian formula is used. This is evidence beyond question that these particular words come from the later experience of the church, not from Jesus' day. *Father, Son, and Holy Spirit* reflects a time when the church had begun to introduce its own experience of God's three ways of being God into its liturgical life. Originally baptism was "into" the name of Jesus only. The Great Commission in no way suggests that Jesus himself ever baptized.

Teaching them to obey all that I have commanded you. This statement points to all of the five discourses of this Gospel as being the divine imperative.

The promise that Jesus will be the spiritual presence of God with the disciples confirms what was promised in anticipation in the name *Emmanuel.*

§ § § § § § §

The Message of Matthew 28

Not in this Gospel, nor in any of the other three, do we see the actual Resurrection. This tremendous event marking the beginning of the age to come remains hidden behind a veil of mystery. At the door of the tomb we must walk by faith, not by sight. Recall Jesus' words to Thomas recorded in the Fourth Gospel: *Because you have seen me, you have believed; blessed are those who have not seen and yet believe* (NIV, John 20:29). We are still called to believe where we cannot "prove," as were the women and the disciples in the Gospel story.

Do not be afraid (verse 5). Rebirth into new life is still and always a frightening experience to witness or to pass through, no less today than at the tomb of Jesus long ago. As at Jesus' birth where the angel said, *Do not be afraid; for see, I am bringing you good news of a great joy* (NRSV, Luke 2:10), so at the empty tomb God still sends assurance with the message, *Do not be afraid.*

Subconsciously we still sometimes try to find Jesus among the dead—among the pages of history, enclosed within the covers of the Bible, in moral codes. We forget that "He has risen" and comes to us as a *living* Spirit.

Where, then, can we "find" Jesus? He comes to us when we go into the world on God's mission, making disciples by faithful witness to the gospel, telling others by precept and example what Jesus said and did. There is where Jesus says he will be with us. The risen Christ is not just a universal spirit like the air we breathe. He is "Maker, Defender, Redeemer, and Friend" to all who join him in his passion, his death, and his resurrection. *If we have been united with him like this in his death, we will certainly be united with him in his resurrection* (NIV, Romans 6:5).

§ § § § § § §

Glossary of Terms

Abel: The younger son of Adam and Eve. His death at the hands of his older brother, Cain (Genesis 4:8-16), came to be considered an anticipation of the death of Christ. Abel was regarded as the first martyr (Matthew 23:35).

Abraham: Israel's first patriarch, the father of the faith of Israel and of the new Israel, the Christian church (8:11).

Angels: Spiritual beings who were thought to be messengers from God (1:20).

Archelaus: Son of Herod the Great, brother of Herod Antipas. For a while, after the death of his father, Archelaus was tetrarch of Judea; but he committed violence against the Jews. Upon their appeal to Caesar, Archelaus was assigned to Gaul in A.D. 6 (2:22).

Arimathea: A village twenty miles east of Jaffa in the hill country northwest of Jerusalem. It is mentioned only once in any of the Gospels as the native village of Joseph, who claimed the body of Jesus after the Crucifixion. He was an official of some kind in Arimathea (27:57).

Babylon: Ancient capital of the empire that rose to its zenith under Nebuchadnezzar, 605–562 B.C. To this empire the Jews were deported at the time of the Exile in 586–538 B.C. (1:12).

Baptism: A rite of purification using water as symbolic cleansing from sin, practiced by John the Baptist but not by Jesus. In the early church it was the initiatory rite for converts (3:13).

Barabbas: The name of the prisoner whom Pilate released in the form of amnesty when he condemned Jesus to die. Mark and Luke make him out to be an insurrectionist. Matthew says simply that he was a *notorious prisoner* (27:16).

Beelzebul: The chief of the devils or Satan (12:27).

Bethany: A small village a mile and a half east of Jerusalem, lying on the eastern slope of the Mount of Olives. Bethany was the home of Mary, Martha, and Lazarus whom Jesus raised from the dead (21:17).

Bethlehem: A town in Judea, five miles south of Jerusalem, ancient home of David the king. Bethlehem was said to be the birthplace of Jesus, son (descendant) of David, who would be the Messiah (2:1).

Bethphage: A tiny village a bit farther east than Bethany. It is from Bethphage that Jesus commences his "royal entry" into Jerusalem at the beginning of the Passion week (21:1).

Bethsaida: A village on the northeast shore of the Sea of Galilee. Jesus condemned Bethsaida for her failure to repent. Some evidence indicates this as the scene of the feeding of the multitudes by Jesus (11:21).

Betrothal: The first stage of the marriage transaction. In the case of Mary and Joseph, Mary was indeed considered Joseph's wife, but he did not know her sexually until after their formal marriage (1:18).

Blaspheming, Blasphemy: Dishonoring the name or the work of God, a repudiation of divine blessing. The scribes accused Jesus of blasphemy (9:3; 26:65).

Blessed, Blessing: Word formulas through which the power of God was expressed (5:1-11).

Bridegroom: A metaphor for Christ as the bridegroom of the church. It is commonly used in connection with the messianic wedding feast, as for example in 25:1-13.

Caesar: The family name of Julius Caesar. His adopted son took the name Caesar Augustus (27 B.C.–A.D. 14) identified in Luke 2:1. Tiberius Caesar (emperor A.D. 14-37) was the first Roman emperor to claim that title. He was emperor at the time of the crucifixion (22:21).

Caesarea-Philippi: A city on the southwest slope of Mount Hermon in what is now Lebanon, 1,500 feet above sea level. It was at one of the sources of the Jordan River. In Jesus' time it was a great center of Graeco-Roman civilization. Here Peter confessed Jesus to be the Christ (16:16).

Caiaphas: Chief priest in the Sanhedrin, the Jewish High Court, at the time of Jesus' trial, according to Matthew 26:57. Another tradition has it that Annas, father-in-law of Caiaphas, was high priest. We have no conclusive evidence. The high priest was appointed by and accountable to Rome.

Capernaum: City on the northwest corner of the Sea of Galilee. Jesus made this city his home during his public ministry (4:13). It is thought that Capernaum was also the home of the disciples Peter and Andrew. The synagogue at Capernaum is mentioned in connection with the healing of the centurion's servant (8:5-13).

Centurion: The Roman officer who commanded a company of 100 infantry in a Roman legion. A centurion supervised the execution of Jesus; he declared Jesus to be a son of God (not a messianic confession), possibly meaning a kind of pagan demi-god (27:54). Earlier, Jesus healed a centurion's servant (8:13).

Chorazin: A city about two miles north of Capernaum. Jesus upbraided Chorazin and Bethsaida for their unbelief (11:21), promising woe to the cities on the day of judgment.

Close of the Age: That time when the present age will be brought to a decisive end by God, and all people, living and dead, and nations will be judged. Then God's new age will begin (28:20).

Cup: A metaphor used by Jesus to signify the experience of suffering and death he would undergo (20:22-23; 26:39). In the Last Supper the cup provides a blessing (26:27).

Curtain of the Temple: The barrier that separated the innermost Holy of Holies in the Temple from the inner and outer courts. It was ripped from top to bottom when Jesus died, symbolic of the end of the former age (27:51).

Cyrene: A Greek city on the north coast of Africa, home of Simon who was conscripted to carry the cross of Jesus (27:32). A large part of the population were Greek-speaking Jews.

Daniel: An Old Testament prophet living in the second

century B.C. His prophecy, Daniel 11:31, was in reality spoken against the king of Syria who set up a statue to Zeus in the Temple in 168 B.C. But it was veiled as a prophecy against the Babylonian King Nebuchadnezzar in the sixth century B.C. Matthew 24 cites it as a prophecy against Rome.

David: The king of Israel and Judea, 1000–962 B.C., to whom all Jewish kings trace their ancestry. The messiah, the earthly ruler through whom the kingdom of heaven would be restored, was to be a son of David (1:1; 9:27; 12:23), who would establish God's rule with incomparable power.

Decapolis: Ten Greek cities in the region east of the Jordan from which crowds came to follow Jesus early in his ministry (4:25).

Demon: Generally understood to be an agent of the devil (Satan). Demons will be overwhelmed and punished in the final judgment. In the meantime they can be exorcised by confronting them with the name of God (9:28-30; 17:18-20).

Denarius: A Roman silver coin worth one day's labor (20:2, 9-10, 13).

Devil: The great adversary of God, believed to entice people away from obedience to God (Chapter 4). God has prepared an eternal fire for the devil and his angels (25:41).

Dove: Often used as a likeness to perfect faith and obedience. Jesus' disciples were to be *innocent as doves* (10:16). The dove was required as sacrificial offering in the Temple in Jesus' time. At Jesus' baptism God's Holy Spirit descended on him like a dove (3:16).

Egypt: One of the great powers of the ancient world on the southeast coast of the Mediterranean. Egypt was the empire from which the Jews made their Exodus in the thirteenth century B.C. At the time of Christ Egypt had become a Roman vassal state. According to Matthew, Jesus' family took refuge from Herod in Egypt (2:13).

Elders: The men of power and important stature, the heads of influential families who controlled the behavior and traditions of the people (15:2; 16:21). Not to be confused with the office of elder in the early Christian church.

Elijah (Elias): A prophet in the ninth century B.C. whose return was to be the sign of the appearance of the messiah (16:14; 17:3; 27:47-49).

Emmanuel (Immanuel): A name given to Jesus in Matthew's birth story (1:23). The name recalls the promise foretold by Isaiah (Isaiah 7:14) that God would deliver Israel from her enemies. It means literally *God with us.*

Field of Blood: According to Matthew 27:8, a burial ground for strangers in Jerusalem, the name based on the incident in Jeremiah 32:6-15. The chief priests bought the field with the money Judas returned after the betrayal of Jesus. Luke tells a different story of how the field came to be called *Akeldama,* field of blood (Acts 1:15-19).

Gadarenes: Name of the people dwelling in Gadara, a Greek city five miles southeast of the Sea of Galilee. Mentioned in 8:28 as the scene of Jesus' healing of the demoniacs among the swine who plunged into the sea.

Galilee: A region of northern Palestine west of the Sea of Galilee, administered in Jesus' time by Romans; the scene of the entire ministry of Jesus prior to his final journey to Jerusalem. Nazareth, Capernaum, Bethsaida, and Cana are all in Galilee. A heavy population of non-Jews lived in Galilee.

Gennesaret: Another name sometimes given to the Sea of Galilee (14:34); also a fertile valley northwest of the Sea.

Gentiles: A name applied to all non-Jewish nations, among whom Israel had to exist and who in the end would be judged as to whether they came to belong to the God of Israel (4:15; 6:32). On their first missionary journey the disciples were told to go nowhere among the Gentiles (10:5). In the Great Commission the disciples are sent to all nations (28:19).

Gethsemane: The olive grove on the western slope of the Mount of Olives facing Jerusalem to which Jesus retired on the night of the Last Supper, and in which he was arrested. The name means literally an *oil plot* (26:36).

Golgotha (Calvary): From the Latin *calvaria,* meaning *skull.* The place outside the wall of Jerusalem where Jesus was executed (27:33).

Gomorrah: One of the cities of the Jordan valley that because of its wickedness fell under the wrath of God (Genesis 13:10). Jesus condemns the towns that do not respond to the disciples' preaching to the same fate (10:15). The remains of Sodom and Gomorrah now lie under the Dead Sea.

Hades: From a Greek word meaning *abode of the dead*. By the time of the New Testament Hades had come to signify a place of punishment (11:23). The older Hebrew concept of Sheol was the destination of life after death, but not a place of punishment.

Heaven: The sky, which serves as a canopy over the cosmic ocean. It was regarded as the crowning glory of God's creation. (See also *Kingdom of Heaven*.)

Herod: A family dynasty that ruled Jewish Palestine as a vassal state of Rome from 37 B.C. to A.D. 70.

Herodians: People loyal to the Herods. In 22:16 Matthew pictures them with the Pharisees in opposition to Jesus.

Herodias: The wife of Herod Antipas, but previously married to Philip, her husband's half-brother. Because John the Baptist condemned her for this violation of the marriage law, she prompted her daughter Salome to ask Antipas for the head of John the Baptist (14:3-12).

Holy Sepulchre: The cave where Jesus was buried in the tomb of Joseph of Arimathea. A Church of the Holy Sepulchre now stands above the supposed cave.

Holy Spirit: In the Old Testament the Holy Spirit is believed to be the power and the means of God's activity. Matthew rarely used the word (4:1; 10:20). In other parts of the New Testament the Holy Spirit is associated with God acting through Christ in the church.

Hosanna: The word means literally *Save us, we beseech thee*. It became a messianic greeting when used by the crowds who cheered Jesus' entrance into Jerusalem (21:9).

Hypocrites (Hypocrisy): When Jesus uses the word (7:5; Chapter 23) he refers specifically to the malice and deceptiveness of the persons of whom he speaks, not the more general understanding of our English word, pretending to be something we are not.

Isaiah: One of the major prophets of the eighth century B.C. in Israel, whose words Matthew quotes from Jesus (4:14; 8:17). Other words, attributed to that first Isaiah, are taken from Second Isaiah, the unknown prophet of the Exile in Babylon in the sixth century B.C. (3:3; 12:17).

James: At least three men named James are mentioned in Matthew. James and John, sons of Zebedee, are two of Jesus' most trusted disciples (4:21; 10:2; 17:1; 26:37). According to 13:55 Jesus had a younger brother named James. Although he was not a disciple during Jesus' lifetime, he became an important leader in the Jerusalem church. Paul includes him among those to whom the risen Christ appeared (1 Corinthians 15:7). A James whose mother witnessed the Crucifixion is mentioned in 27:56.

Jericho: A city of almost unparalleled antiquity at the southern end of the Jordan River where it flows into the Dead Sea. The Jericho of the New Testament was built by Herod the Great, who made it his winter capital. Nearly a thousand feet below the Mediterranean Sea level, the climate was mild in winter, stifling in summer. Two blind men cried out to Jesus in Jericho (20:29-34). It served as a Roman garrison town in the time of the Jewish Wars, A.D. 70.

Jerusalem: A city sacred first to the Jews, later to the Christians, and still later to the Muslims; located on the central plateau 2,500 feet above sea level. The road from Jerusalem to Jericho drops over 3,500 feet in less than twenty miles. David made the city the Hebrew capital, which it remained, save for the interruption of the Exile, 586–538 B.C. In Matthew Jesus visited Jerusalem and the Temple only once, in the last week of his life. Here he was crucified and raised from the dead. Luke and John record earlier visits to the city.

Jesus: Personal name of the one whom Christians call "the Christ." The chosen one of God. The Jewish form of the name was Joshua or Jehoshuah, and meant *Yahweh will save* (1:21).

John the Baptist: A prophet whose father, Zechariah (not the prophet), served in the Temple (Luke 1:5). The Gospel tradition in Matthew and Luke calls John's mother Elizabeth, cousin to Mary the mother of Jesus. John's preaching roused the nation to repentance; multitudes came to the Jordan to be baptized for cleansing. Jesus was baptized by John (3:13-17). *Jonah:* Old Testament prophet whose name is given to the tale of the prophet who preached in the pagan city of Nineveh. Jesus contrasted the repentance of the people of Nineveh with the lack of response to his own preaching (12:38-42).

Jordan: The most important river in Palestine, rising in the north from the slopes of Mount Hermon; it empties into the Dead Sea eighty air miles to the south, over 200 miles by the river's course. To the Jordan River Jesus came to be baptized by John, at what point no one knows for sure (3:13-17). The Jordan flows through the Sea of Galilee.

Judah: Bethlehem was located in the land of Judah, territory taken by the tribe of Judah when the Israelites entered Palestine after the Exodus. Bethlehem, southeast of Jerusalem, according to tradition, was the birthplace of Jesus (2:1), fulfilling the prophecy of Micah 5:2.

Judas Iscariot: The betrayer of Jesus. A man from Kerioth in southern Palestine. Judas was the only Judean among the twelve disciples.

Judea: The territory formerly called Judah in southwest Palestine. It was almost 45 miles square, extending from the Dead Sea to the Mediterranean coast, as far north as Joppa, over to the Jordan River and down to the Dead Sea (2:1; 24:16).

Kingdom of Heaven (Kingdom of God): These two expressions are virtually interchangeable in the Gospels, although Matthew prefers kingdom of heaven to kingdom of God. Jesus spoke, saying the kingdom of heaven had already come (12:28). But the term also refers to the age to come. Wherever God rules in a person's heart or among people now or at the end time—this is what the kingdom of God is like.

Leaven: Except in 13:33 where Jesus likens leaven to the kingdom of heaven, where the good influence of the Kingdom leavens the whole company, leaven has evil connotations in both the Old and New Testaments. Leaven works because of fermentation and it breeds corruption and debases life. In this sense Jesus warned against the *leaven* of the Pharisees (16:11).

Leper, Leprosy: One of the skin diseases so endemic in that part of the ancient world. The disease causes the skin to erupt in rough scaly patches; in extreme cases limbs degenerate and drop from the body. A leper was considered unclean and was banished from all human contact. Lepers came to Jesus for healing (8:2); he sent out his disciples to *cleanse lepers* (10:8). We even see Jesus in a leper's house (26:6).

Little ones: In Chapter 18 Jesus speaks specifically of children for whom the disciples are to have the greatest care and respect. The term can also refer to those new in the faith who need solicitous care.

Mammon: A term Jesus used in the Sermon on the Mount for wealth, property, or profit. He warned the disciples that they could not serve both God and wealth (6:24).

Mary Magdelene: A woman from Magdala on the west shore of the Sea of Galilee. She appears by name at the Crucifixion (27:56) and at the tomb to discover the Resurrection (28:1). Presumably she was in the group of women who followed Jesus. Some legends have it that she was a penitent adulteress. This interpretation is based on the doubtful ending of Mark's Gospel (Mark 16:9).

Master: When used as a title for Jesus it meant *chief*, one who leads with authority. It is found often in Matthew and serves as the term for the head of the disciples.

Moses: The one through whom God made the first covenant with Israel at Mount Sinai. Jesus refers to Moses as the giver of the law. In the Transfiguration Moses appears with Elijah, symbolizing the Law and the Prophets (17:3).

Mount of Olives: The mountain, part of the range of mountains running north and south through Palestine, which overlooks Jerusalem to the west. Jesus sat on the Mount of Olives when he delivered the words of the Apocalypse, Chapter 24. The Garden of Gethsemane lies on its lower western slope (26:30).

Naphtali: The sixth son of Jacob in the Book of Genesis, father of the tribe of Naphtali. Their territory was west of the Jordan, northwest of the Sea of Galilee. Matthew quotes Isaiah 9:1-2 when he announces that Jesus began to preach (4:12-16).

Nazareth: A hill country village in Galilee, halfway between the Sea of Galilee and the Mediterranean Sea, the home of Mary and Joseph where Jesus grew to manhood. He was widely known as Jesus of Nazareth (26:71). Nazareth was situated not far from a main international highway at Sepphoris.

Nineveh: The capital of ancient Assyria. In the story of Jonah the prophet was sent to preach in Nineveh. Jesus contrasted the repentance of the people of Nineveh with the failure of the generation to whom Jesus preached (12:41).

Outer darkness: A description of Hades (Hell) to which the *sons of the kingdom* were cast because they did not believe or were worthless servants (8:12; 22:13; 25:30).

Pharisees: A party among the Jews whose principal task was keeping the letter of the law and preserving the ancient traditions. They believed in the resurrection where people were rewarded or punished for their behavior in this life. Late in the first century they strongly opposed the emerging Christian church. Jesus directed his continuing and often scathing judgments against the hypocrisy and failure to honor the ancient prophets in their own times (see particularly Chapter 23).

Pigeon (Dove): The word means literally to *moan* or *moaning bird*. The *dove* was always used as a metaphor for the Spirit of God (3:16). Pigeons were also the most common sacrificial offering in the Temple (21:12).

Pontius Pilate: Roman procurator (governor) of Judea, A.D. 26–36. He condemned Jesus to death (27:2-26).

Praetorium: The residence of a Roman provincial governor. The Roman Praetorium in Jerusalem was the judgment hall for Jesus' trial before Pilate.

Priests: Ones who were set aside to administer the affairs of

152   MATTHEW the Temple. Chief priests occupied a higher place in the Temple hierarchy, the high priest being chief above all. The chief priests were the ones who actively sought Jesus' death (26:3).

Prince of Demons: (See *Satan* or *Beelzebul*).

Prophets: Men who spoke to the nation for God: *Thus saith the Lord.* Jesus called John the Baptist the greatest of them all (11:11); he condemned the scribes and Pharisees because they would have shed the blood of the prophets had they lived in the prophets' days. Matthew cites more than thirty texts from the prophets that Jesus fulfilled.

Queen of the South (Sheba): Matthew makes reference (12:42) to the visit of the Queen of Sheba, south Arabia, to King Solomon (1 Kings 10:1-13) to show that a pagan queen sought wisdom from Solomon. Now something *greater than Solomon* was here (Christ himself).

Rachel: Rachel was Jacob's second wife, the mother of Joseph and Benjamin. Matthew quotes Jeremiah 31:15, referring to the Jews being carried into exile. Many generations after Jacob and Rachel the slaughter of the children at Bethlehem seemed to Matthew a fulfillment (2:16-18).

Ramah: A town north of Bethlehem, the traditional site of Rachel's burial. The identification of Rachel with Ramah may well be erroneous (Jeremiah 31:15; Matthew 2:16-18).

Righteousness: Faithfulness to a covenant between partners, between God and Israel, or among people. Thus when Jesus says, *Blessed are those who hunger and thirst for righteousness* (5:6), he is saying that such people want above all else to be faithful and obedient. He also admonishes the disciples that their righteousness must exceed the righteousness of the Pharisees (5:20). It was fitting for Jesus to fulfill all righteousness, that is, every condition of the covenant, when he went to be baptized (3:15).

Sadducees: The party of the priesthood in Israel. They controlled the affairs of the Temple and were threatened by Jesus' disturbance in the Temple (22:34).

Salt: An essential in preserving food and thus a necessity of life. Jesus tells his disciples that they are to be the salt of the earth—a requirement for life (5:13).

Samaritans: Dwellers in Samaria, north of Judea. Historically Jews and Samaritans were enemies, giving the principal point to Jesus' parable of the Good Samaritan (Luke 10:30-36). Jesus instructed the disciples going out on their first mission, *Enter no town of the Samaritans* (10:5).

Satan: The head of all the devils (demons). He is the enemy of God, over whom God's ultimate victory will be won. Jesus recognizes Satan speaking through Peter (16:23). Jesus also knew Satan as his tempter in 4:1-11.

Scribes: They were closely identified with the chief priests in the Temple. Jesus links them with the Pharisees in his condemnation (12:38; Chapter 23).

Sea of Galilee: A freshwater lake in the Jordan River, three and one-half miles long and three miles wide. Around the lake Jesus' Galilean ministry took place. Here lay the towns associated with that ministry: Magdala, Bethsaida, Chorazin. On this lake Jesus sailed with his disciples through the storm (8:23-27).

Sidon: A city on the Mediterranean coast north of Tyre. Jesus went there when he withdrew from Galilee (15:21).

Sign: Jews in Jesus' day believed God gave outward evidence of divine purpose generally hidden from casual observance. People looked for signs to know God's intention (24:3). Jesus warned against seeking for signs (12:39).

Silver, thirty pieces: The amount of *thirty pieces* (26:15) is from Zechariah 11:12, where the prophet speaks of a worthless shepherd being paid a wage of thirty pieces of silver. This may have been symbolism for Judas, intended by Matthew.

Sodom: A city condemned by God for wickedness (see *Gomorrah*).

Solomon: The name is derived from *Shalom*, meaning *peace*; Israel's third king, son of David, celebrated for his wisdom.

Son of Man: Sometimes a title for Jesus (17:9; 26:24). In some cases it is a name for the heavenly judge coming at the end time, not identified with Jesus (10:23; 25:31).

Synagogue: The place where the Jewish community gathered to worship and study. Jesus frequently taught in their synagogues (12:9; 13:54).

Syria: The region from which people came in great numbers to find healing in Jesus' ministry (4:24). The name here refers to the region north of Galilee.

Talent: In Jesus' time a talent was a unit of weight measurement. It was also a monetary term for 6,000 drachmas, roughly equivalent to $1,000, an extraordinary sum in those days (25:14-18).

Tax Collector (Publican): The men who collected the poll and land taxes for the Romans. Many were Jews; they were despised for being agents of the hated Roman Empire. Jesus associated with them (11:19), ate at their tables (9:11), and declared that they would go into the Kingdom before the chief priests and elders (21:31).

Tithe: The tenth part of a person's property given to support the priest or the Temple. Jesus condemns the scribes and Pharisees for meticulous attention to tithing *trifles* and neglecting *justice, mercy, and faith* (23:23).

Tyre: A famous Phoenician seaport on the Mediterranean coast. Jesus withdrew from Galilee to Tyre (15:21). Jesus declared that Tyre would have repented had he done there what he did without avail in Chorazin (11:21).

Wise Men: In the story of Jesus' birth (2:1-12), they were probably members of a priestly caste somewhere in Persia who interpreted dreams and observed heavenly signs.

Zebulun: The tenth son of Jacob. The tribe taking his name occupied a comparatively small territory adjacent to Naphtali in central Galilee. This was the scene of the beginning of Jesus' ministry (4:12-17).

Zechariah: One of the prophets in the period following the Jews' return from exile. Matthew's interest in Zechariah lies in two passages of his prophecy which he saw fulfilled in Christ: Zechariah 9:9, quoted in Matthew 21:1-11; and Zechariah 11:7-14, quoted in Matthew 27:3-10.

Guide to Pronunciation

Abel: AY-bell
Abraham: AY-brah-ham
Archelaus: Ark-keh-LAY-us
Arimethea: Air-ih-muh-THEE-ah
Babylon: BAA-beh-lon
Barabbas: Buh-RAA-bus
Barachia: Bah-rah-KEE-ah
Beelzebul: Bee-ELL-zeh-bul
Bethany: BEH-thuh-nee
Bethphage: Beth-FAH-jee
Bethlehem: BETH-leh-hem
Bethsaida: Beth-SIGH-duh
Caesar: SEE-zar
Caesarea-Philippi: Sess-ah-REE-ah-FILL-ih-pie
Caiaphas: KIGH-ah-fas
Capernaum: Cah-PER-nah-um
Centurion: Sen-TOOR-ee-un
Chorazin: Koh-RAH-zin
Cyrene: Sigh-REE-nee
Decapolis: Dee-CAP-oh-liss
Denarius: Deh-NARE-ee-us
Egypt: EE-jipt
Emmanuel: Ih-MAN-yoo-ell
Gadarenes: GAA-deh-reens
Galilee: GAL-ih-lee
Gennesaret: Jeh-NEH-sah-ret
Gethsemane: Geth-SEH-mah-nee

Golgotha: GOLE-gah-thah
Gomorrah: Guh-MORE-ah
Herod: HARE-ud
Herodias: Heh-ROH-dee-as
Isaiah: Eye-ZAY-uh
Jericho: JEH-rih-koh
Jerusalem: Jeh-ROO-sah-lem
Jonah: JOH-nuh
Jordan: JORE-dun
Judah: JOO-dah
Judas Iscariot: JOO-das-Iss-CARE-ee-ot
Judea: Joo-DEE-ah
Leaven: LEH-ven
Magadan: MAH-gah-don
Mammon: MAA-mon
(Mary) Magdelene: MAG-dah-len
Moses: MOH-zez
Naphtali: Naf-TAH-lee
Nazareth: NAA-zeh-reth
Nineveh: NIH-neh-veh
Pharisees: FARE-eh-seez
Pontius Pilate: PON-shus-PIE-let
Praetorium: Pray-TORE-ee-um
Sheba: SHEE-buh
Rachel: RAY-chel
Ramah: RAH-mah
Sadducees: SAD-yoo-seez
Samaritans: Sah-MARE-ih-tons
Satan: SAY-ten
Sidon: SIGH-dun
Sodom: SOD-dum
Solomon: SOL-oh-mon
Syria: SEER-ee-uh
Tyre: TIRE
Zebulun: ZEB-yoo-lun
Zechariah: Zeh-kah-RIGH-uh

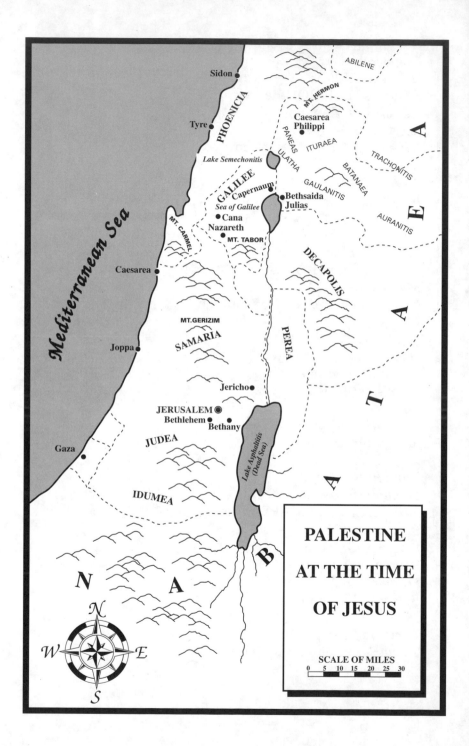

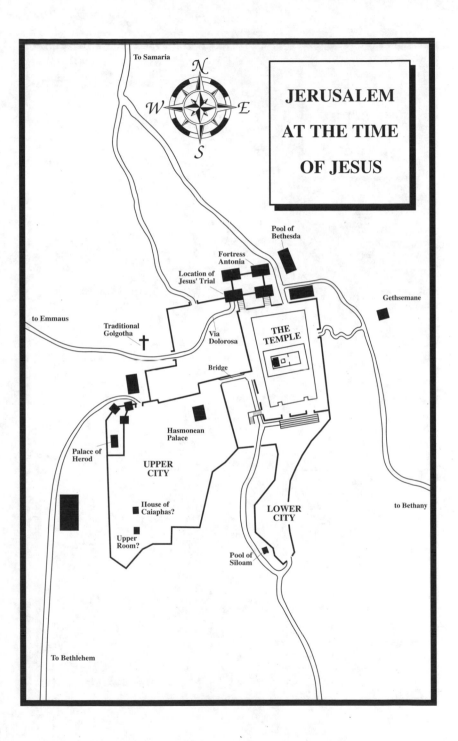

To Samaria

N
W E
S

JERUSALEM
AT THE TIME
OF JESUS

Pool of
Bethesda

Fortress
Antonia

Location of
Jesus' Trial

Gethsemane

to Emmaus

Traditional
Golgotha

Via
Dolorosa

THE
TEMPLE

Bridge

Hasmonean
Palace

Palace of
Herod

UPPER
CITY

LOWER
CITY

to Bethany

House of
Caiaphas?

Upper
Room?

Pool of
Siloam

To Bethlehem

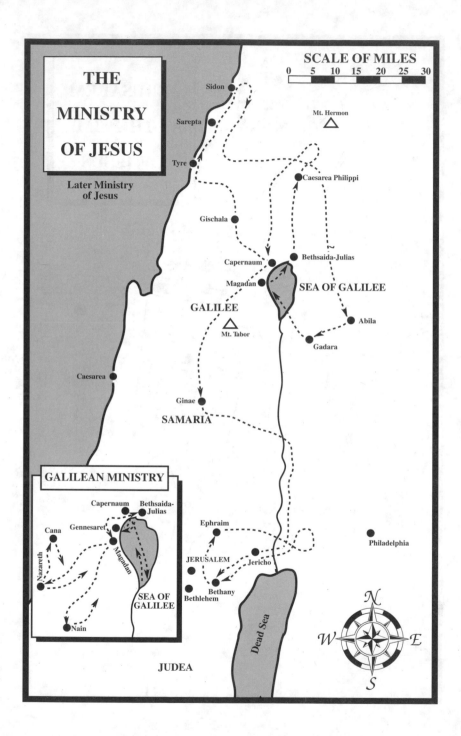